APPALACHIAN
REVIEW

VOL. 50, NO. 2
SPRING 2022

FEMINISM IS FOR EVERYBODY.
—bell hooks

EDITOR
Jason Kyle Howard

BOOK REVIEWS EDITOR
Emily Masters

STUDENT ASSISTANTS
Skylar Bensheimer

MANUSCRIPT READERS
Katherine Scott Crawford & Patti Frye Meredith

ESTABLISHED IN 1973
PUBLISHED QUARTERLY
by Berea College
CPO 2166
205 N. Main Street
Berea, Kentucky 40404
www.appalachianreview.net

Electronic submissions only at www.appalachianreview.net

Distributed through a partnership between the University of North Carolina Press and Duke University Press. Basic subscription price: $30/year for individuals, $60/year for institutions. For subscription requests and inquiries, visit the magazine's website, email subscriptions@dukepress.edu, or call 888-651-0122 (toll-free in the US and Canada) or 919-688-5134.

CONTENTS

COVER PHOTOGRAPH
bell at Apollo Pizza by Wesley Browne

EDITOR'S NOTE

JASON KYLE HOWARD

L ast December, the world lost an icon. This magazine lost a champion, a guiding voice. I, and so many others, lost a friend.

When I think of bell hooks, so many memories come to mind. Lunches at the Dinner Bell in Berea. Singing "Ring My Bell" and "Gloria" in the dark when the electricity had gone out after a spring storm. Her love of music; how she adored Meshell Ndegeocello's album *Pour une Âme Souveraine: A Dedication to Nina Simone.*

In 2015, bell and I collaborated on a special issue of this magazine that was devoted to her work. Over lunch at an Indian buffet, we discussed what we would include. Her critical theory and scholarship was so well known, and I wanted to highlight her creative work. She agreed, and then she suggested we use an excerpt from her unpublished novel *Sister Ray Seeks Salvation*. "That Sister Ray's a mess," she laughed, devouring a samosa. "You'll have to tell me what you think about her."

What I thought, when I received her recommended excerpt a few days later, was that she was right. Sister Ray *was* a mess—but in the best possible way. Sister Ray was bell, or at least a lightly fictionalized version of her. Consider: in the chapter, Sister Ray is at a party. People are dancing, talking, seducing and being seduced. Sister Ray is studying the room, her keen eyes lighting on different people and one man in particular—the man she wants. Although she is a photographer, bell makes sure the reader knows that Sister Ray is something more. A detective. "Ray," she writes, "was primarily interested in portraits. She certainly did not give a damn for photographs of landscapes. It was the taking of the portrait that was like seduction. She was interested in seduction."

bell herself loved to size people up. She had often taken their measure even before an introduction, and even when she liked, and loved, the person, I think she would still periodically test them. Sometimes for fun, to provoke, and other times for something more consequential. To teach them something. This chapter from Sister Ray, I felt, was one of those tests. It was steeped in character interiority, in physical longing, in sex, and since *Appalachian Heritage*—as the magazine was known then—had often, before my editorship, shied away from publishing work about physical desire, I thought she was prodding me to see what I would do with the piece. If I would publish it, if I would defend it in the face of any resistance. She was teaching me in that moment, reminding me yet again of something she had said when I took over as editor: "That magazine needs shook up." She was right, of course, and that had been part of my mission all along—to transgress the notion of what was considered Appalachian, of *who* was considered Appalachian. To push readers to think more deeply and broadly about what and who counted.

In this region, in this country, in this world: bell counted. I still can't believe that seven years after her tribute issue, I am assembling this one, a different kind of tribute, alone. But what a group of writers, all of whom knew and loved bell. Crystal Wilkinson has allowed me to reprint her remarkable essay "I Am a Writer Because of bell hooks" that originally appeared in *The Atlantic*. Paul Gilroy, Qrescent Mali Mason, Darnell L. Moore, Gloria Steinem, and Dr. Linda Strong-Leek have generously contributed the pieces they wrote for Berea College's memorial service. Wendell Berry and Silas House have shared the remarks they gave when they were invited by bell's family to speak at her Celebration of Life in Hopkinsville, Kentucky. Our cover image is of a mural at Apollo Pizza in Berea, created by Matthew King and Keena Sparks with bell's blessing.

In addition, there are other voices in this issue who are continuing bell's tradition of deep character examination, of questioning. They are writing their truths, and they are writing to transgress against systems, identities, ideologies, and traditions that have been imposed upon them. And they are doing so with the love about which bell so often spoke and wrote.

bell hooks was fierce in her ideas and beliefs, and she also set a welcome table, as evidenced by the blessing she commissioned from the Reverend Rachel Small-Stokes that bell made sure was invoked at each event of The bell hooks Institute:

> *To all who enter these doors: blessings upon you, for you are friends. You who are weary of oppression and seek to cast your eyes upward, you who are buoyed by privilege and seek to bring others to the surface of justice, you who are affected in ways you haven't even yet identified; you who are Appalachian, Affrilachian, Fabulachian, or from far away; you who are feminist, womanist, mujerista, queer; you who are heteronormative, racist, patriarchal, but seek a new way; you who question or who come confused; you who are writers, educators, poets, scholars; you who have been dragged here by others; you who have dreamed of visiting—you are friends. You are welcome. May this be a place of blessed conversation, of dismantling of old systems and building up of new. May you teach, and may you transgress. May you brave the words you thought you could not say and hear those you never imagined you could tolerate. May you live and be formed by this sacred community—curious, courageous, candid, and constructive—as you speak your truth and hear another's. May you be blessed by this place, and may this place be a blessing.*

And may we all continue to read bell's remarkable, searing work, and may we all continue to be challenged, revealed, and transformed. ■

I AM A WRITER BECAUSE OF
BELL HOOKS

CRYSTAL WILKINSON

listen little sister
angels make their hope here
in these hills
follow me
I will guide you

—bell hooks, *Appalachian Elegy:*
Poetry and Place

For all the things that bell hooks was—one of the foremost Black intellectuals in the world, renowned feminist, author of more than forty books, revolutionary cultural critic—and all the places she lived, she was still Gloria Jean

Watkins from Hopkinsville, daughter of Rosa Bell and Veotis. There is no doubt that her entire body of work was shaped by her homeplace and that when she found her voice, she helped a generation of Black Kentucky women writers find ours too.

Though bell often wrote of her "wounded childhood," she was also influenced by her ancestors, like her great-grandmother Bell Blair Hooks (from whom she devised her pen name) and others who taught her to, in the words of Toni Cade Bambara, "draw up power from the deep." bell grew up in the Western part of the state, near the Tennessee border. In *Belonging: A Culture of Place*, she explains that her spirit of resistance was nurtured by rural Black agrarians who valued self-reliance and self-determination above all else. "When we love the earth, we are able to love ourselves more fully," she later wrote in *Sisters of the Yam*. bell often spoke of the loss she felt when her family left the hills to move into town. She called this longing her "first deep grief." The significance of our Kentucky roots—the wounds, the salve—was among the things bell and I talked about after we became friends.

Though I settled primarily on fiction, my work, too, looks back and remembers. My people, real and imagined, gather strength from the Bluegrass. I grew up in the foothills of south-central Kentucky, where nature was abundant, where I was free to roam the creeks and knobs. Like bell's people, my grandparents grew gardens and tobacco and tended animals. They relied on white folks for little. I, too, have written about nature's capacity to heal, especially for Black women, and know that bell was homesick for that balm.

When I met bell, in 1993, she was already an acclaimed writer and theorist. She had lived away from Kentucky for decades. I was a part of a mighty enclave of Black women that included Nikky Finney, Kelly Norman Ellis, Donna Johnson, Joan Brannon, and Daundra Scisney. Some of us were native

Kentuckians; others had moved to Kentucky for jobs or to study. Among us were a grocery-store clerk, a government worker, a jewelry maker, a student, a filmmaker, and a new professor trying to define ourselves. We knew that more than anything, we wanted to tell our stories.

Since bell's passing, the six of us who were there at the beginning all agree that something was already pulsing inside us that caught speed and shifted when she returned home to speak at a writers' conference that year. We'd gathered at the Robert H. Williams Cultural Center on Georgetown Street in Lexington to listen. My then-six-year-old twins sat cross-legged on the floor. It was October, but it was hot. The small room was brimming with excitement. The audience, at bell's insistence, was an eclectic mixture of women from every corner of the community, not just traditional academics.

I was a single mother of three, fresh out of a toxic relationship, unhappy with my public-relations job. bell had a way of turning the concepts and ideology of feminism into brilliant common sense. For the first time, in that crowded room, I connected feminism with my lived experience. bell was a rousing call for radical self-love. She was charismatic. She had the lilt and cadence of a preacher. She made us laugh. She had finessed her accent, but still I heard bits of Kentucky in her voice that reminded me of all the women I loved from back down-home.

None of us can remember how it happened, but Kelly, Daundra, and I ended the night in bell's hotel room. The conversation made great leaps from the inner well-being of Black women to liberation to straight-up gossip. We were giddy, changed. We had held communion with bell hooks. She had treated us like we were her girls. The next night, she gave a huge lecture on the University of Kentucky campus surrounded by throngs of people, but we'd already been privately anointed. After she returned to New York, those of us who had attended the conference began to hold sister circles. We confronted our fears, were tender with one another, became deeper critical thinkers.

Over the years the circle waned, but we all kept writing. Some of us published books or made films. Some of us became professors, but I think we are all teachers, passing on what we learned from bell.

By the time I took a position as writer in residence at Berea College, where bell also taught, she and I had become friends. I accepted the job, in part, because bell was there. She invited me to her house. We broke bread. We talked about love. We talked about Black liberation and family. We reminisced about our Kentucky girlhoods. We were friends, but I never stopped learning from her. She got irritated when I called her teacher or mentor. "Friend," she corrected me once, when we were onstage in public conversation. I never reminded her of October 1993, but she will forever be my teacher.

I am a writer because of bell hooks. I am a feminist because of bell hooks.

bell showed us that all things were possible for rebellious, bookish Black girls. She reminded us that no matter the prevailing stereotypes of Kentuckians (white, illiterate, poor), no matter the unfinished business of eliminating, as she put it, the "imperialist white-supremacist capitalist patriarchy," Kentucky was also a culture of belonging. It was a landscape of thought, memory, imagination, renewal, and connection. She taught us that you can be a Black visionary intellectual from Kentucky and forge a voice of defiance amid—and in order to heal from—segregation, racial hatred, voicelessness, and separation from nature.

Since bell's passing, the five women and I who experienced that night have talked by phone and text. Kelly, a poet and professor, texted me: "She taught me I could be a feminist, a teacher, an activist and a woman on my own terms." When I spoke with Joan, who is a healing drummer, filmmaker, and activist, her voice cracked. "Time gathered with Black women is sacred." Though I hadn't spoken with Donna, a writer and consummate bibliophile, in years, we talked for almost four hours. From bell, she learned "to value our sense of place as Kentucky Black women." Daundra was at work when I videochatted with her. Having lost her twenty-five-year-old daughter this year, she is sick of death. "I'm not supposed to be on the phone," she said. Then she laughed: "Let them fire me after thirty years." She was an undergraduate when we first met and is the youngest among us. "bell taught me that I can be myself," she said. "Talk back, no apologies for who I am." When I called Nikky, she was washing dishes. "Girl, this is the best time," she said. We paused and sighed in disbelief. A shared quiet reached from South Carolina, where she teaches now, back here to me in Kentucky. "I needed bell hooks," she later said in a text, "in order to fully rise into all the women I hoped to one day be. She was a raging, loving river of permission."

In her preface to *Belonging*, bell said, "Memories offer us a world where there is no death, where we are sustained by rituals of regard and recollection." We Kentucky women of the Sister Circle of 1993 thank you, bell, for encouraging us, for helping us become writers, for loving us steady and strong. We've cried. We remember. ■

ON NAMING
AND LESSONS LEARNED

QRESCENT MALI MASON

I have been thinking a lot about grief and love, having recently lost three of my most beloved and influential Black women elders, beginning with bell in December of 2021 and then my paternal grandmother, Gloria Evadne Atherton on March 18, 2022, and four days later, my paternal aunt, my Auntie Karen Marie Mason.

I have been thinking about how difficult and inspiring it has been to really come to grips with how someone you love deeply can be loved as deeply by anyone other than yourself and that this person might have loved others just as deeply, in ways and moments that you will never experience, but in ways that have felt as much like a communion as yours. This has been one of the most surprising aspects of the grief experience I'm having now: to come to terms with the breadth of my loved ones' love with others.

I first came to knowledge of bell hooks as a student at Spelman College. I read *All About Love* and attended a talk she gave there in 2004, where she mentioned something offhanded and shocking about anal sex and I, prude that I was at the time, decided I was *good on that, lady.*

I later relied on her heavily in my dissertation work on Simone de Beauvoir, Black feminism, and the erotic, but can't say that I had any strong desire to know her. I respected the fact that she was a Black woman philosopher who took the subject of love seriously and was courageous enough to write about it directly.

When I applied to the job at Berea, bell's connection to the college was unclear to me, so I was embarrassed and underprepared when she turned up on my computer screen during my Skype job interview, asking me the meaning of the phrase "feminism is for everybody."

I must have responded well enough somehow because I got the job and she invited me and my mother—who she always insisted on referring to as "cute mom"—to the opening of The bell hooks Institute in 2015, and she introduced me to people as if she already knew me well and we got to sing songs in the dark with Laverne Cox when the lights went out at the reception at the dean's house, who had llamas. I think she took a shine to me because of our shared love and respect for

Simone de Beauvoir, who I knew she looked up to and read as a young woman. It might have been for that reason that she insisted, every time she introduced me to someone, on calling me a philosopher, even though I was teaching at Berea in what was then the Women's and Gender Studies Program and is now The bell hooks Center.

When I moved my partner at the time from Philadelphia, where we had bars and he had a growing and bright future as a blues-rock musician, to Berea, Kentucky, I honestly didn't know what I was doing and why.

I told myself there must be some grand lesson I was supposed to learn directly from bell herself. At the time, I convinced myself that it was a spiritual lesson, as I knew her work had been heading in that direction for a while.

Once in Berea, I eagerly accepted any invite to bell's house, hoping time after time to sit at the feet of a wise feminist sage and soak up her wisdom and brilliance. What I found, largely, to my shock and spiritual chagrin, was a slight, sly, childlike-voiced Black lady sitting on a black leather couch, talking shit. Talking shit about every thing and every body. I quickly came to learn that most anything said to bell might then be repeated to anyone else, including but not limited to the man who cut her yard and the woman who sold mushrooms at the farmer's market.

After a year or so, she finally told me to come by at a specific time to become a part of "Group" and I started going over her house every Tuesday afternoon, meeting with various numbers and variegated mixtures of local women from Berea to talk about the challenges we faced as women here. Always, when I was a part, it was my sister-friend Adanma and me, sneaking off afterwards to her house a few doors down to smoke and debrief the day's session, often to her husband Shane's amused annoyance.

I must say that when I left Berea to take my current job in the Philosophy department at Haverford College outside of Philadelphia, I couldn't figure out what lessons I had learned from bell. I had met a lot people. I had taught her work. I had read as much as I could in the archives. I had come to love her. And I had asked her a lot of questions. A LOT of questions. But when I left, I still felt I had failed in getting my lesson, especially if it was supposed to have been one of the spirit.

I've realized now that some lessons you only really get in retrospect and sometimes when someone's presence becomes a physical absence, that's when the lessons actually begin.

So here are a few that I have learned and continue to learn from bell:

The first is the value of naming, of naming systems, of naming oneself. bell believed in the power of the word. So much so, as we know, that for the majority of her adulthood she chose to be called by a name that she herself had taken up, one that connected her to her maternal line, one that she insisted would buck the conventions of the English language in order to take the focus off of herself and put it on the message. We disagreed over and over again about the efficacy of the term "intersectionality," which I held was useful for its ambiguous ubiquity and which bell said, for those very reasons, could not do the same crucial work as her chosen "imperialist white supremacist capitalist patriarchy," which was clear to name and call out those specific systems from which we must work to free ourselves.

I now realize, in her insistence to call me a philosopher over and over again, that bell also wanted me to name myself. She writes in her essay "Beauvoir and Bell: True Philosophers," "In the racially segregated world of my growing up, the only time I heard the word 'philosopher' was when I was mockingly called by that sobriquet when I was being deemed too 'serious' about the world of ideas. Although I never told anyone, it gave me great pleasure to be called a philosopher, when I learned that the root meaning of the word was 'lover of wisdom.'"[1]

She wanted us to share that claim to wisdom, that claim to philosophy. She wanted me to announce myself, to take up the name that had been so often denied to Black women thinkers like us.

In August 2020, our first pandemic summer, bell allowed me to spend a week with her, recording between twenty minutes and an hour and half most days, of interviews with her about her work and her life. Each day, me and my lover-cum-audio engineer sat with her in her home, bringing her offerings of trinkets and food. Her health was not good so my friend Kevin, a healer, sent me with some honey and a comb and had me bring her specific flowers. Despite this, though, bell was mischievous in her answers to my questions, making me work hard, often seeming to suggest that the answers had already been given. She was always like this, redirecting the conversation if it bored her and pointing everyone back to her work.

I have also come to learn that coming to know someone is trying to build a context around the complexity of their being. Here are things that I witnessed bell struggled with while I knew her: forgiveness, regarding and honoring the feelings of others, loneliness, suicidal ideation, keeping people's confidences/secrets, a sometimes miscalibration of the meaning and persistent need for "talking back," not always accepting and receiving love and care offered to her. I meditate, with bell as an ancestor, on these struggles, some of which I share, and ask for the wisdom to heed her example in its fullness, maybe even to enact some of the lessons she didn't or couldn't.

bell was generous. She gave of her time and she gave, I am coming to understand more and more, as more and more people describe to me how close they feel to her, how she saved their lives, she gave of herself. I think often about all the projected lovelessness and invisibility and silences that bell shouldered in her mission to rid her life of hers as an example of how we might rid our lives of ours.

When I received a few calls in December that bell's time was coming close, I hopped in my car and drove from Philly to Berea, hoping to have the opportunity to ask bell more questions. I thank Dr. Valeria Watkins, bell's sister, for allowing me to spend time with bell in her last days, as she faded from consciousness. I tried to sneak in at least one more question. I asked, "So what have you been thinking about?" Like always, she answered in the most bell way possible: "Life." And then, despite the fact that it labored her to be in conversation, asked me "Whatever happened to that lover-cum-audio engineer?"

I can now see that when we were chatting shit in her living room, I was, in fact, only beginning to get my lesson. I thought I was looking for a lesson that I could recognize as such, but instead I am only really coming to understand the things I actually did learn from her. That they were, in fact, lessons of the spirit.

Someone suggested that I should leave you with a takeaway, some kind of praxis, what hearing me talk about bell should encourage you to do. I can only suggest that you do as I am committed to doing: continue to learn your lessons from bell. David Whyte writes that "the death of anyone close to us is always a form of salutation, a simultaneous goodbye to their physical presence and a deep hello to a more intimate imaginal

1   hooks, bell, "Beauvoir and Bell: True Philosophers," in *Beauvoir and Western Thought from Plato to Butler*, ed. William S. Wilkerson and Shannon M. Mussett (Albany: State University of New York Press, 2012), 229.

relationship now beginning to form in their absence."[2] If you are one of the many thousands of people who formed a relationship with bell, whatever form it took, whatever kind it was, continue to nurture that relationship. Continue to engage her work and to teach her work and to be critical of her work. Continue to hear her voice talking shit in your ear. Continue to support the efforts of those who, like myself, are committed to protecting and continuing bell's legacy. And when given an opportunity to do so, name yourself. ■

2   Whyte, David. *Crossing the Unknown Sea: Work as A Pilgrimage of Identity* (New York: Riverhead Books, 2002), 46.

IN REMEMBRANCE OF BELL HOOKS:

ON BEING HUMAN

DARNELL L. MOORE

I met bell hooks in October 2014. At the time, I still held an image of her as an iconic writer rather than an enfleshed Black woman full of desire and deep feeling. She was, after all, one of the most consequential feminist writers and intellectuals of our time. And like most well-known, widely-read, and celebrated figures, I connected to the life-changing words that she penned in her books without realizing that her words were connected to a beating heart. bell was more than an avatar deserving of veneration.

Seven years ago, one of the organizers charged with curating her residency at the New School extended an invitation to join bell in a public conversation on manhood, alongside educators Oman Frame, Ron Scapp and Kurt Voss. To say that I was ecstatic to be in the same room with her would be an understatement. Before we walked out of the green room and into the packed lecture hall, bell jokingly asked, "You sure that you aren't gay?" I laughed and affirmed that I was, in fact, a homo. But I remember that moment as revelatory. As I grew to learn, bell flirted and made jokes and gossiped and offered sharp cultural criticism and wrote conversation-starting books and loved and lusted and was erotic and spiritual and transparent and complicated because that was the stuff of her humanness.

As much as she wrote and talked publicly about love with a poignant and graceful brilliance, she was a writer/thinker who was only able to write with such stunning power about a variety of themes because she first wrestled with the ways such themes emerged in her own life. On another occasion, a few years after the New School talk, I visited the institute that bears her name at Berea College in Kentucky. After we finished our talk, we went back to her house, where we chatted about everything from the business of publishing to relationships.

I was stunned when she revealed that none of her books had ever made a bestsellers list or that she hadn't received big advances for her works because she understood that the payback would come in the form of royalties. She schooled me that day. She told me about her writing regimen—how she reads one or two books a day and how she wakes up early to write. I silently wished that I possessed half of her will. She reminded me to write only that which moved me because that is what she did. And she shared stories about some of the relationships that she most cherished and even lamented her then current lack of intimate partnership. I was single at the time and connected with her desire. I let her know that I didn't want to write about a love that I didn't experience in real ways, in real time, in my own life. She understood. No amount of books or celebritydom can fill the inner wells of desire that even the sharpest of writers do their best to explicate on the page. The writing is, at best, a proximate step towards that which is imagined. And that is one of the reasons I respected her—because she imagined for herself and for those of us who read her.

I want to remember bell's imagination and her wide grasp of cultural theory among much else. But I also want to remember her laughter and her honesty. I won't forget when I was honored to share an author's table with her at the Tucson Festival of Books in 2018. As we chatted over dinner, opposite a table post with a picture of our books on it, a white woman table-mate interrupted our dinner and conversation to get in a few words with bell. Before too long, bell looked past me and into the eyes of the woman and said, "Do you mind? I am trying to eat my dinner and don't want to talk right now!"

I gasped. bell was unafraid, and I thought about how freeing it would be to be more honest, even if such honesty hurts, because honesty can lead to transformation, which is what bell modeled in writing and her living. She labored to ensure that Black feminist theory was connected to a praxis and way of life. Radical honesty, on the page, meant the radical living of the words she wrote in her life.

I want to remember bell's living. How she traveled and sat before crowds of people when her body allowed her to over the last several years, in spite of illness. How she would refer to herself, the writer, in third person. How she would *spill* tea with a casual ease in a way that was so reminiscent of a favorite aunty as our mutual friend, DaMaris Hill, once described her antics. I remember the story she told about building the bell hooks Institute and how her good friends, like Beverly Guy Sheftall, supported her while a few well-known scholars didn't think it was worthwhile to support her effort at all. I know that some of those same scholars might be remembering and celebrating her today because that is what we do. We often only recall the good after the worst takes our people from us. But the gift that we can offer each other in this life or the next is a celebration of the full breadth of one's humanity and her story.

Several days before bell passed, some of her friends traveled to Berea to surround bell with presence and love. I traveled to her home along with Stephanie Troutman and DaMaris Hill. Stephanie and I sat on opposite sides of bell, Stephanie holding one hand and me the other. "You still look good," bell mumbled. I giggled through my sadness because I knew that bell's spirit was still animating her mind and body. I sat silently because I couldn't believe that a person who had become a force in the world of ideas, public intellectualism, and popular culture criticism was soon to transition. I didn't know what to say besides, "I love you." And I am forever grateful to have heard her reply, "I love you, too."

Even in her last days, she taught me a lesson about humanity, namely, the truth that we should damn sure **LIVE** until we no longer can. And should we ascend, there are the records of our living. In her case, there are the words and moments, which if read carefully, will offer a glimpse into that which interlocking systems of power try to unravel—our relationships to self and to one another. And ain't that a Black feminist lesson from someone who talked and dreamt and wrote all about love? ■

THE CAPTAIN
OF ALL SHE SURVEYED

GLORIA STEINEM

I've been asked to speak about my dear friend bell hooks today, but I have to say it's not part of the natural order of things. She was way younger than I, so this should be the other way around. But to begin at the beginning, I think I first met bell when she was teaching at Yale in 1992 because she had the daughter of a dear friend of mine as a student, and it was clear, right away, that she was special because the students were fighting to get into her class. How often does that happen? Then she moved to New York, and we saw each other more. She had an apartment in New York, and we spent a vacation together on Cape Cod, on Martha's Vineyard.

My funniest memory of her is shopping on Cape Cod. She was a fierce, fierce shopper and tireless. She enjoyed buying inexpensive things and small bits of jewelry and scarves. That was something I recognized from my own childhood when neither of our families had that much money, so going into a store, even an inexpensive dime store, was a kind of heaven.

What then and now inspires me most about her writing is her insistence on the value of love, even though love is a very devalued, cheapened, misunderstood word. But, nonetheless, she took it seriously. She wrote about it, and she showed that it was possible in life, despite patriarchy, despite racism, despite divisions, that a freely chosen relationship was possible. That was revolutionary because it meant freedom—true, true freedom. Once, when bell was not so well and she was confined to her couch in Berea—she, of course, attracted and was loved by, cared for, by faculty members, students, family members, and friends—she reminded me of a captain of a ship on her couch in the living room, communicating with distant shores, the captain of all she surveyed even though she must have been worried about her health, as we all were. And because of her sitting there on that ship of her own couch, she brought so many disparate people together over the years.

If I had to pick one of her books that was my favorite, I'd pick *Ain't I a Woman?* because bell takes on the idea that a revolution can exist for women, which is not a popular idea. And in *All About Love*, she dares to see a revolution in which such a trivialized word as love becomes deep and important and powerful because it can bridge all hierarchies. She also said, "You can teach by being in the world as much as by the work you write"—and that is quite a big sentence when you think about it, because she demonstrates that teaching, learning, all of it is really democratic. We teach by everything we do, by every word we say. We are open to learning by listening. But she was fierce when she described the adversary to you. She would always say the "white, capitalist, racist, patriarchy." And she would say it together all the time, so it definitely included everything. Therefore, she understood that given all those hierarchal, exploiting forces, love is a radical act, both to love ourselves and to love other people as unique individuals.

Sometimes I think to myself in particular situations, or any situation, "What would bell do?" Then I try to do it. One literal example is that we were both invited to speak at a big conference, a women's conference that gradually fell apart because of divisions among the organizers and never happened, but bell never gave up. She went on having meetings in her hotel room with all of us late into the night trying to make it happen. That's who bell was. She was the patient organizer as well as the speaker, the star, the writer. She did it all. To also follow bell is understanding that neither gender nor race nor class exists. They're all inventions, so we can un-invent them. We can uproot them and begin to see each other as unique individuals.

Sometimes I think that the world is divided into two kinds of people: those who see the world as divided into two kinds of people and those who don't. Like bell, I'm doing my best to see the world as undivided and to approach each person as a unique individual, and that is why she used the often-devalued word, love, and made it strong, made it meaningful, made it serious, made it empathetic. By love, she did not mean romance. I think in love, you want what's best for the other people. In romance, you want the other person. It's much more possessive. bell definitely knew the difference. She knew how important it was to feel loved and to feel valued as your unique self. And it was important and life-giving to her, so she understood that that was true for everyone else, too. Love has been a devalued word, but bell gave it back its value. ■

ON BELL AND
GLORIA

PAUL GILROY

ell hooks has already been widely, rightly, and righteously lamented as our Hipparchia, our Beauvoir, and so much more. I have no doubt that process will continue as her extraordinary work finds new publics and makes new readerships across the planet. bell's world-changing contribution will ensure that mourning and affirming her will continue when and wherever love, critique, and the pursuit of freedom are combined and invoked by rebels, dissidents and sufferers seeking justice, autonomy, recognition and rights, but also by people seeking to form communities, enhance mutuality and find authentically democratic, pre-figurative modes of dwelling: the necessary home she wrote about so consistently and provocatively.

Her enormous and rich body of work cannot be reduced to the dimensions of a footnote in the histories of US feminism and the Black movement. It is a tantalizing and prematurely-concluded chapter in the annals of human liberation, in the healing of our species and our world.

My companion Vron Ware and I were greatly privileged to know both bell hooks and Gloria Watkins well. For me, those two were never quite the same person. Their contrasting characters overlapped and spilled into one another, but they seemed, in some ways to be antagonistic. The conjoined mentalities of bell and Gloria could express divergent orientations and priorities. The difference between them was not Manichaean. It defies any simple split between public and private selves. It was not just bell hooks's *writing* which troubled that gendered, bourgeois line. Her conduct troubled it, too.

It is Gloria that I want primarily to remember and grieve for today. I speak not only for myself, but for my immediate family who were all changed by her entanglement in our lives, and also for her various friends in London—Karen, Isaac, Mark, Luke Daniels, Philip Dodd and various others living and dead. My responsibility to that remote constituency, that vagrant history and those happy memories, means it is important that today's larger act of public mourning acknowledges Gloria's travels, transits and homes away from home. Those were experiences that altered her outlook profoundly. You may catch a glimpse of this from the record of her adventures—loves, intellectual exchanges and gifts; her teaching, intervening, and guiding discussion and debate. The TV shows she made in the UK and the Netherlands provide a glimpse of those activities. She had happy stays at the Penn Club in Bloomsbury. And she spent precious time with people she visited in other parts of Europe who also today grieving for her: her dear Marieke in Amsterdam; Rosi, Anneke and the other Gloria in Utrecht.

I want to affirm Gloria's value to Vron and myself as a surrogate parental figure in the lives Marcus and Cora. Most precious to me are memories of the happy time she passed in our homes, particularly in this garden touched today by spring's first breath.

I am so glad that Gloria led me astray. She challenged me to think and say things I wouldn't previously have been bold enough to express in ways that I would never have dared to employ. My life was enriched by her fearlessness. Her open approach to life, her principled refusals and calculated transgressions taught me that we had only to be loyal to our best visions of how healing could take place, how the world might be made more hospitable and habitable: firstly for black women and girls, but for all the survivors and victims of trauma and violence which were always conceptualised on multiple scales. How the world might be made safer for the exploited, the wretched and the downpressed, and better for all kinder, gentler and therefore vulnerable souls committed to following the difficult, dangerous paths of mutuality, peace and love.

I would like us to remember Gloria not only as a revolutionary thinker and an iconic commentator, but as a compulsive writer who broke their addiction, as pathological reader *and* a joker. We should accommodate her Eshu spirit as a disruptive and playful presence as well as a supremely productive one.

I've been thinking about the fact that she told me several times James Carr's "Dark End of The Street," a queer anthem if ever there was one, was her favourite song. It meant a lot to me that she was a music lover (especially of Prince and James Brown). Her enthusiasm for the dancefloor should not disguise the fact that she was also as a *moralist* of an interesting and in some ways a peculiar sort: somebody who could orbit Baldwin's attack on sentimental writing, while being herself an unabashedly sentimental writer.

To my mind, even though she loved cashmere, Gloria was an essentially ascetic person. Someone who, like many others in these troubled times, sometimes struggled to uncouple herself from the glamour and distractions of white-supremacist, *consumer*-capitalist, patriarchy.

I cannot unsee the absurd red mink coat that thrilled her in her Lil' Kim phase. I wonder what happened to it? She was someone who was intermittently drawn towards the trappings of a celebrity culture that she knew full well was toxic to her health and to her many special gifts and insights.

I met Gloria in 1990 on an academic visit to the US. She was hanging out with Michelle Wallace and Cornel West. I was taken aback when she cornered me and said that she had come to find me there because she had sensed a kind of kinship. Obviously, I knew her writing, but my reading had been insufficiently alert to pick up the connections from her words on the pages which were exceeded immediately, in every way, when she spoke them in her whiny, southern voice. We all know that she was a Soul Rebel, funny, scurrilous, and acute in ways that her beautiful, brilliant writing could not hint at.

At that point, her notoriety was growing and her absolute intelligence, the restless radiance of that one-off mind, was making some lesser people distrustful, envious and hostile towards her which took another toll. After that, I visited her in Oberlin where we sat with her colleague and friend Calvin Hernton and she first articulated what would later become a refrain. What she laughingly dismissed as the "halls of academe" were not hospitable to her future-making, world-changing capacity to re-envision, heal, and explain the world anew—to communicate on a different frequency.

I loved Gloria's mind, her eloquent critical consciousness, her ability to read not just texts, films, and images, but *everything* and to speak that lucid critique thoughtfully in ways that people of all kinds could hear and possess.

She was, perhaps above all, a teacher who built a unique, practical and political pedagogy on foundations supplied to her by Paolo Freire, by her fundamental feminist commitments and a complex, hybrid spirituality in which aspects of Buddhism and Afro-baptism were braided with a yearning for tranquility and a deep reverence for nature— though not for other people's dogs—that had been refined for during her time in California as well as her return to Appalachia.

Now, we must face the sorrow of living without Gloria and the difference that she made. For me, this new situation of loss means not striving to follow her example which is obviously impossible, but seeking in the spirit of love she helped us to appreciate, to bring her wild creativity along with us. I fear we will need that stubborn spirit with its ethical commitments to dialogue and mutual attentiveness more than ever in the trials that surely await us. ■

ELEGY FOR A
GENIUS

SILAS HOUSE

bell was my friend for twelve years, and for the last nine of those we lived a few blocks from each other in Berea.

I keep thinking about the way bell made people belly-laugh. She wore a proud, mischievous smile after she had said something particularly something. She was incredibly blunt. But the longer I knew bell the more I began to see it more as direct honesty and I respected that. Once she decided to have an impromptu dance party at her house—she loved dance parties—but when it reached a certain hour she shouted out, "Okay, party's over. Everybody leave!" In bell's way of thinking it was much kinder to let people know when she was tired than for her to sit there and be tired of *them*. Being around someone so incredibly honest sometimes requires a thick skin but I loved that I always knew where I stood with her.

bell loved dinner parties with people she liked. She always sat at the head of the table and told story after story. Through the course of the tales she often wept. I would guess that bell was moved to tears just about daily. The best people I know are this way. She felt everything very deeply. Anyone who has read her work is aware of this great empathy she carried to the point of it being painful to bear.

bell loved going to the movies and she particularly enjoyed the films of Pedro Almodóvar. When my husband and I saw Almodóvar's controversial film *The Skin I Live In* a few years ago with her, we went across the street to a restaurant where we drank wine and talked about it for three hours. To hear her talk about any movie was a lesson in how to observe, how to feel, how to experience a piece of art. She devoured art and her house was full of everyday kinds of art, framed photographs, towers of books, stacks of CDs. A bowl of oranges assembled beneath a painting of Frida Kahlo, a gathering of ceramic heads that she kept under the window in her living room to catch the morning light. She had chairs and tables painted in bright colors, especially red. She adored bright colors.

For awhile she and I attended the same church, where she listened intently to the sermon and always wanted the music to be more "lively". Sometimes after church we would sit on my porch and analyze some of the scriptures or discuss Buddhism and Christianity. Or just gossip. I cherish those Sundays.

For a long stretch of the twelve years I knew bell, she wrote every day and perhaps even more monumentally, she read an entire book every day. She did not merely scan these books; she read them carefully. She took young writers and feminists and activists under her wing without much fanfare. She gave our work to others without telling us.

I'm focusing on all that was wonderful about bell here but she was also a human being. She was complicated and often contrary. Sometimes we disagreed about issues or people and even though I almost always deferred to her, I knew that bell would not respect me as her friend if I didn't let her know how I felt in these situations. Always she listened to me, she considered what I was saying, and she appreciated being challenged, even when it miffed her. I think nothing I know about her makes me respect her more than that.

When you went to bell's house sometimes you'd find a group of students there. She'd be leaned over on her couch because of the almost-constant pain she experienced for many years and they'd be sitting in the floor or a scattering of kitchen chairs. Other times you'd find people like Cornel West, Laverne Cox, Emma Watson, or Gloria Steinem drinking tea and discussing everything from fashion to Palestine to the latest Spike Lee film. She spoke to these celebrities the same way she spoke to the students, and to me, and everyone.

We often went out to eat together. Once we stopped at a little country cafe and she decided to go speak to every person seated there. She touched all of them—farmers and construction works and children—shaking their hands or patting their shoulders, and talked to them about her love of cars or Goodwill shopping. When we sat down I laughed and said, "I swear, you must know everyone in this restaurant." She said she didn't know a single one of them. "But I wanted each one them to have to speak to a Black woman today."

She was so interesting and beautiful and magnificent. I loved the way bell used her hands. They floated before her sternly, elegantly, as she spoke in her steady, calm, yet forceful way. I think often of her hands in motion. I think of her voice, which was so soft for such a large presence. She often referred to herself as "a little country girl from the hills." She was proud of that, even though aspects of it held great pain. She was troubled by Kentucky but she also loved it fiercely. I think of that little girl often these days, about to burst with all of that intelligence and fierceness and bravery in the hills of Christian County, Kentucky.

The first time I met her she told me we were going to be friends, and we were. When I was with her, I always knew I was in the presence of a genius. I always felt loved when I was with her. And I loved her back. ■

.

SHARED
ALLEGIANCE

WENDELL BERRY

A good many years ago, when I heard that bell hooks was speaking favorably of me and some of my work, I thought that was remarkable. It seemed remarkable, of course, because the racial division is so prominent and so much in the way.

But then I met bell hooks. We sat down and talked, unseriously with some laughter, and also seriously. This was a friendly conversation, which means that as we talked our points of view freely converged and diverged as honesty required. And I realized that her approval of me—which I think was somewhat limited, for it was intelligent approval—though it probably was rare, was not remarkable.

The two of us, as she had seen, belong to a kind of people who can speak to one another with understanding across even the headline divisions of race and sex. This is a kind of people rapidly disappearing at present, but a kind nonetheless valuable and needed: country people, agrarian people, who come from places they conscientiously know, suffer and love as "home." It is because of this that I so often read bell hooks with the sense of being, not only spoken to, but spoken for.

To affirm publicly in our time, as she did, the value of our shared culture and allegiance required courage. It required, I think, the same courage by which she spoke always as and for herself. My respect and my gratitude for this give the measure of my sorrow for her absence and my sense of loss. ■

LOVE
IS AN ACTION

DR. LINDA STRONG-LEEK

bell hooks was my friend. I don't say that lightly. Our friendship was something I rarely talked about to people who were not close to me because I never wanted to be one of those people who wanted something from her—who were biding their time until they made the big "ask" for what they wanted all along. Our friendship happened naturally. It started with a once a week lunch meeting, and evolved into two-three times a week lunches, coffees, phone calls. I never expected that one of my best friends in the world would be this feminist icon—this person who taught me so much about life, and love, and self-care. bell and I shared many things—a love of good, old-fashioned Southern food, especially my macaroni and cheese, sweet potato pies and greens, and my special baked beans. We also loved hot fudge sundaes from Dairy Queen, and often shared one because bell loved to share food with those she loved. I can't believe sometimes that she loved me, but she did, and I loved her.

bell and I had many things in common—we were both sassy little Southern girls who talked too much—who talked back—who loved to read. We both had five sisters (I have two brothers, while she had one—her beloved Ken), and we both loved music—gospel music, old school R&B, good country music—so much music. We both loved beautiful men—men who were not just beautiful on the outside, but the inside as well. And because of bell I learned to love to dance—I was, and still am one of those Black people who does have any natural rhythm—but with bell, I danced and laughed and found my voice. She helped me to fully embrace my Black feminist self.

Like most good friends, bell and I also often disagreed. For instance, I still love *The Color Purple*—it is one of my favorite books, and bell hated it. I agreed with Michelle Obama's decision to focus on her daughters when Barack became President, because, as the mother of Black daughters myself, I worried more about how the world would react to and treat my amazing, articulate, intelligent daughters than almost anything else. I understood Michelle's decision. I loved dogs, and she hated and feared them, so whenever she came to my home, I would put the dog outside so that she would feel safe. We argued, we laughed, and we cried together when we lost loved ones. I was with her in Puerto Rico when she shook the National Women's Studies Association with her powerful speech. I remember our amazing week at Martha's Vineyard—she took me there for my fiftieth birthday—when we walked to the Inkwell to watch the beautiful Black women gather together to swim, and when we were walking back and she stopped a stranger to drive us back because she was tired. I remember when we were in the airport traveling, and people would walk by and say, *is that bell hooks?* and she would just smile.

I remember how she lit up when she saw babies and small children—she loved babies and children. I remember most of all that small voice—that powerful voice—the way she challenged all of us to live our lives out loud, to speak our truths. She taught me that I, we, all deserve to be loved with a capital L—love as an action—love as a verb. I loved my friend, and I miss her, and I still cannot believe that she is gone.

We will keep bell's work and memory alive. She worried about all of the Black women writers who died, and whose memories seemed to fade into the distance—every time another Black women writer left us, we would talk about her project—The bell hooks Institute—and how she wanted the Institute to live on long after she was gone. So I proudly announce today that Berea College, in conjunction with The bell hooks Estate, will reopen The bell hooks Institute in the next year to honor the life, legacy, and love, of my dear sister-friend, black feminist scholar-icon, bell hooks. ∎

WILDFLOWERS

Gettysburg, 2020

If I am going
to spend ten dollars,
let it be on a giant
bouquet of wildflowers,
from a farm in the neighboring town.

After all, it is my due date, late
July, my family and I
having frittered the morning
blueberry picking
and eating, inside an arc
of blue rows, after weeks
of no rain.

The farmer herself
sold them to me, a day old
on discount, colors spewing
from the bucket like a spring—
crimson, clementine,
sky blue, fuchsia.

In town, a militia
with guns. Howling acidic
things, while my loam-hued children
bring the blooms home,
bestow some on our neighbor,
a few on the grave,
the rest on the table—
a sunflower, dahlias,

bright as beating hearts,
and I change (belly brimming)
into my cotton dress
while you sweat and huff
in your thick leather.

I wish you would
come inside
where it's cool.

I wish
you would admit
the abundance.

In the middle of this drought,
I wish you would come, put down your guns,
and drink.

SHANNON ST. ARMAND

AN *APPALACHIAN REVIEW*
CONVERSATION

JOCELYN NICOLE JOHNSON

Timely: that's but one word to describe
Jocelyn Nicole Johnson's electric debut *My
Monticello*, a collection of stories and a novella
that bears witness to the white supremacy of
both the past and present. Set in and around
Charlottesville, Virginia, where Johnson lives
and writes, the book centers on Black and
Brown characters as they navigate the notion
of home, both as a physical and spiritual place:

the single mother who dreams of buying her first home, the mixed-race woman who changes her name to escape oppression, and in the title novella, a diverse group of neighbors—led by a descendant of Thomas Jefferson and Sally Hemings—who turn to Monticello in the face of racist violence.

Critically acclaimed upon its release last autumn, *My Monticello* recently received the 2021 Weatherford Award in Fiction, given to the work of fiction that "best illuminate[s] the challenges, personalities, and unique qualities of the Appalachian South." Johnson spoke with essayist, fiction writer, and *Appalachian Review* contributor Monic Ductan about *My Monticello* and its upcoming adaptation for Netflix. The conversation has been edited for length and clarity.

■ ■ ■

MONIC DUCTAN: Of the stories in *My Monticello*, which is closest to your heart?

JOCELYN NICOLE JOHNSON: I included these stories in the collection because they are *all* close to my heart and related to one another in their shared exploration of home, longing, dislocation, and loss. The story that is probably closest to my way of being (though not my lived experience) is "Buying A House Ahead of The Apocalypse," a slim investigation of existential dread woven through with pop culture references, Black girl hair considerations, and aspirational shopping, all in the form of a bulleted to-do list.

MD: The first story in your collection, "Control Negro" feels very timely in regards to the protests against police violence toward Black men in particular. Were you

Jocelyn Nicole Johnson

inspired to write that story by learning about any recent events? Elijah McClain? George Floyd?

JNJ: "Control Negro" was inspired by a local incident that predates the murders of Elijah McClain and George Floyd. In 2015, here in Charlottesville, a Black University of Virginia honor student, Martese Johnson, was bloodied by uniformed Alcohol Beverage control officers along the crowded strip of restaurants and bars adjacent to his campus. The incident, caught on video, and the resulting heartache echoed a long tradition of excessive force wielded by institutions toward Black and brown and poor people. In my dark story "Control Negro," I looked at one father's twisted attempts to escape this intergenerational trauma.

MD: Your book is a novella and a collection of stories. Can you say a bit about why you arranged it that way? Did you set out to write a book of stories or did it just kind of happen organically?

JNJ: I was writing what I thought were stand-alone stories when I began to recognize a pattern. Most of my stories were set in Virginia and explored some aspect of belonging. Seeing this, I started to imagine a set of stories like pins pressed into a map of my home state. I wrote the novella "My Monticello" last, but because it pulled at so many of the threads of the earlier stories and even echoed a few of their phrases, I felt it belonged *with* them.

MD: Can you say a bit about your inspiration for writing the book? Who or what inspires you?

JNJ: These stories, by in large, were inspired by my view of the world between 2015 and 2019—moments of trouble, longing, and hope—everything from seeing children seek power in a classroom to watching a deadly white nationalist rally wreak havoc on my town of Charlottesville in August of 2017. I often write when I am bewildered by the world, to avenge something, or try to figure something out.

MD: I read recently that your novella, "My Monticello," is being made into a Netflix movie. Can you tell us more about that? Do you have details about when it comes out or about the narrative approach to telling your story on film?

JNJ: Yes, the novella "My Monticello" is currently being adapted into a film for Netflix and is in the screenwriting phase! The challenge of these kinds of adaptations is to make the internal *external* and visible. My small contribution as one of the executive producers is to advocate for the big ideas of the story: In this case, a celebration of feminine and communal power in the face of racial and environmental reckoning.

MD: What do you see as the most helpful piece of writing advice you've received?

JNJ: I often think back to when Aimee Bender, who was leading a workshop at Tin House that year, drew a line on the whiteboard to illustrate how much we should shift our stories in reaction to comments from our classmates. On one end of the segment, she wrote something like, "Change Everything" and on the other, "Change Nothing." Then she placed a dot toward the middle but slightly closer to Change Nothing. She talked about how, when getting feedback, a writer should be open to critique and suggestion, but not *too* open. What I came away with was an affirmation that, as artists, we had to value or own instincts and intentions.

MD: Do you have any rules for writing?

JNJ: Try to enjoy it. Try to keep at it.

MD: Could you recommend some writers you enjoy? Writers from which you've learned the most?

JNJ: I'm drawn to writers who draw from different genres to get at truth, writers like Octavia Butler, Charles Yu, and Nana Kwame Adjei-Brenyah. I'm also a fan of nuanced moments made up of sharp sentences, as seen in writers like Toni Morrison, Richard Wright, Jhumpa Lahiri, Junot Diaz, Ruth Oseki, Garth Greenwell. I love the short story form, and have been moved by collections from writers like Danielle Evans, Jamal Brinkley, Cal Angus, Te-Ping Chen, Dantiel Moniz, and many others.

MD: You're a Virginia native and a person of color. Do you ever write from your own personal experiences with racism or white nationalism?

JNJ: As I mentioned earlier, I absolutely write in response to what is happening in my community and in my country, including my experience of race, racism, and white nationalism. In this collection, I've written in response to conversations overhead, a travesty caught on video, and a public spectacle of hate. Even when I'm imagining, I'm writing from what I've seen and heard and felt.

MD: There's been a lot of talk recently about people of color and the publishing industry. Do you have any advice for other writers of color in terms of breaking into the industry or finding a wider audience?

JNJ: Read widely. Be open, but cultivate your own sense of intention. Learn to love your own words, and if not your words, then at least the process of putting them down and honing them. Remember, you cannot control the world, but you can choose your words, and the ordering and reordering of them. Meanwhile, find community (a trusted group of writers, a mentor or two). When you're ready to send your work into the world, look for partners that believe in your work and your intentions— journals, agents, editors, a team. Try to appreciate it when any reader connects with your words, and don't pin your joy on some external goal of a certain kind of publication. Publication has its own anxieties, even under the best of circumstances. For me it took many years and three agents before I published my first book at age fifty. No one can wait that long for joy. Find joy in your words, in the process of making and trying.

MD: Congratulations on winning the Weatherford Award for Appalachian fiction. I know writers are always labeling themselves and being labeled by their readers. Do you see yourself as an Appalachian author? A Southern writer? If you were to apply labels to yourself or your writing, what would they be?

JNJ: Thank you! I'm honored to be recognized by the Weatherford Award and described as an Appalachian writer. I could also be called a Southern writer, a Black writer, an American writer, a writer of literary and low-key speculative fiction. By and large, I appreciate being encircled by multiple descriptive labels that invite readers in, hopefully with each label complicating and enriching the next.

MD: I watched your GMA [*Good Morning America*] interview with Robin Roberts and she asked about the

rally in Charlottesville and at one point you said you were inspired by those events to write *My Monticello*. Could you describe your hometown? What do you love about it? What do you dislike? How has your home place influenced your writing?

JNJ: My experience of my home state isn't necessarily about what I like or dislike. Virginia has been the ground beneath my feet, where many of my loved ones live, where my son was born. Virginia is where promises have been made and broken. An early engine for this collection was thinking about the ways Virginia, and America, feel both like home and *not* like home, to me. I wanted to explore and share my longing for an incontrovertible home for my nerdy, artsy, Black girl body, and the insights that come from straddling that border. ■

MARCO POLO

we're private people as you know   we've told

the kids but not the grandkids   the kids all say

it's not my fault   I've done nothing wrong nothing

to bring this on   it's the   uncertainty

I hate   and the waiting   the grandkids are

getting ready to go back to school   we've said goodbye

for the summer but until we know something for sure

we don't see the sense in telling them   I've asked

your mother to "run the beads"   that's what Dad called

the rosary   she's taken his place   she's become

my spiritual teacher   we consider her family

that makes you family too   we asked her

to include you in the news   here is a photo

of my joker of a husband floating in the pool

we haven't dug yet   they'll break ground on it

soon   the stakes you see outline its kidney shape

and there's Joe lacing his fingers behind his head

stretched out on the green grass of the lawn

he's mown for all these years   he's taking it

hard   next summer when the grandkids play

in the pool   we'll have to remind them of the rules

of Marco Polo   the little ones can't help

but cheat   they open their eyes and kick their feet

hard but still can't reach the swift-swimming teenagers

so tempers flare   when the one who's It

calls MARCO I'll call POLO and let myself be caught

I hope I'm here to call POLO   I hope I'm here to let

the youngest boy's soft fingertips touch the wet

skin of my arm   I hope I can still swim

easily away   I hope I have a choice   for once

I hope I take my sweet time diving under escape

untouched come up for air on the other side

I hope I'm still here   I hope I get another year

of wear from the bathing suit I bought last spring

I hope it fits   I hope the grandkids never know

the reason for my fear   I hope they never know

this fear   if you talk to them please don't

tell them don't upset them   please

keep us in your prayers

MARISA P. CLARK

BLUE RIDGE
BOBBY

CAROLINE McTEER

*The door opened and Johnson Gibbs stood solidly
in it. His blue eyes were very bright. There was
full sunlight now and it made a burning glare on
the snow. Against this harsh light Johnson's figure
loomed black, black as velvet, blackly burning,
and his voice sounded deep and hollow:*
"Well, Jess, are you one of us or not?"

—Fred Chappell, *I Am One of You Forever*

The day after my grandfather Bobby died, I drove with my sister from Charleston, South Carolina to Bakersville, North Carolina, a town of not-quite-500 along the Tennessee border. We stopped for food in Asheville, parking by a bank of purple asters. I threw open the car door to catch that first mouthful of mountain air. It tasted as sweet and clean as the water in the creek on Bobby's property. I had made this trip many times. Season after season, I had seen mountains appear like great blue shadows in the distance, my anticipation rising as they came close enough for me to see the trees that covered them. That feeling was the same when I was four as when I was twenty-four. The nearer the mountains were to me, the nearer I was to my grandparents. There had been twenty-six years of trips to the mountains, and Bobby had been at the end of all of them. This time he wasn't, and never would be again.

Bobby had spent the last weeks of his life consolidating the family land in Bakersville, getting it all in his and MeMe's names so that it would be with their children and grandchildren forever. Already, the pressure was on: which one of us would choose to build a home and make a life in the mountains; who would carry on Bobby's passion and give meaning to his final act? None of us grandchildren had such a plan.

I found it all depressing beyond belief. For one thing, Bobby bought a big piece of the land from a stingy nephew who charged him far more than what the land was worth—I'm told. MeMe claims that being treated so poorly by a family member drove Bobby's stress levels up and played no small part in that final heart attack. She was furious when said nephew came by the trailer to say he sure was sorry to hear about Bob.

When it was him who caused it to come about, my mom said when she told the story, clucking her tongue and taking up the Appalachian-speak of her childhood, as she always does when her mind or body are in the mountains. It didn't seem to occur to her that there may have been a more nuanced version of the story than the one she'd heard. In the same way that some people are straight-ticket voters, Mom always sides with her parents. Before Bobby died, Mom had been threatening not to vote in the upcoming presidential election, which was still months away. She wanted Hillary Clinton to win, but didn't think she could vote for her, "on account of how it would upset Daddy."

Bobby was a Trump supporter, to my great bitterness. My family took his final political affiliation as an example of how Fox News has taken advantage of the elderly. "I don't know how someone as smart as Bobby could be taken in by all that," my sister Shayna would say, "but you just think about how much he cares about environmental preservation and you know he doesn't actually side with Trump. And you see how he was with his neighbors getting deported."

I did see. Bobby and MeMe were very close with a family of immigrants from Mexico who lived next door to them, and they remained in touch after the family moved to Florida. There, they were caught without papers. Bobby wrote a letter on their behalf to the immigration judge, and he told Mom to write one too. (She did.) "If his neighbors had been from the Middle East," Shayna said, "it would have been the same."

Would it have, though? In my experience, Bobby was selectively prejudiced. He was educated about the history of Cherokee people in the area of North Carolina where he lived, and neither he nor my mom minced words about how cruel and unjust white people had been toward them in the 1800s, when we displaced Indigenous people from their homelands in the Southeast to current-day Oklahoma, killing thousands along the way. Bobby, a union-man, was a long-time Democrat (since FDR) until Obama won the Democratic primary in 2008. At that point, his views took a hairpin turn. I'd love to attribute the change in Bobby's political affiliation to anything other than Obama being Black, but to do so seems absurd.

On one visit, I saw a magazine on the trunk next to his sofa, whose cover had a particularly nasty and ghoulish caricature of Obama. I didn't say anything: MeMe begged us not to talk politics with Bobby, because of his heart. When my sister and I tried, it never went well for us. Bobby died at age eighty-nine, and maybe I should account for some level of mental frailty in my estimation of him. But he seemed sharp until the very end, and I couldn't find it in me to absolve him for what he'd believed.

■ ■ ■

The night we arrived, I stood with my brother Evans on the gravel driveway across the street from our grandparents' trailer. To the left, we could see the land Bobby had grown up on, and directly to the right was the land our grandmother MeMe had grown up on, where, as a child, Bobby would take food from his family to hers during the Great Depression. By starlight, Evans and I could see the garden from which we'd both had the best food of our lives: butter beans or crowder peas with thick chunks of sliced tomato and cornbread on the side, green beans cooked with just a little sugar, salt, and canola oil, watermelon that had gone straight from the garden to a bucket of cold water, then to a stepping stone to be sliced open and eaten only yards from where it was harvested.

"I think she hasn't had enough watermelon," Bobby said one time with a little grin, speaking both to and about me. I was fourteen, crying inconsolably on an occasion when my parents wouldn't let me have my way. At the time, it came across as good-natured teasing, but in retrospect, I think he was actually trying to problem-solve: when it came to relationships, food was Bobby's main currency.

This is my first memory of my grandparents, from when I was three or four: They came to visit and MeMe grabbed me up in her arms with a flurry of excited exclamations. Then she turned a black garbage bag upside-down, dumping its contents. It was full of things she'd collected for me at yard sales: VHS tapes, ruffled play-clothes. Bobby stood in the corner of our kitchen with his hand on his hips, an almost bashful smile, and a box of sweet potatoes. Bobby was one of eighteen children. Mom figures that his mother ladling food onto his plate was the closest he ever got, as a child, to individual attention.

I sometimes feel guilty that my connection with Bobby wasn't more profound when he was living, but then I remind myself how much I tried. We had both tried, and in that trying

I sometimes feel guilty that my connection with Bobby wasn't more profound when he was living, but then I remind myself how much I tried.

had found some true understanding of each other despite our dissonance. I started the tradition of exchanging letters with Bobby. At fourteen, I knew somehow how much that would mean to him, and I also knew that the letters must be addressed just to him, and not also to my grandmother, with whom I've always had an easy and close relationship. And Bobby was one of the first people to say I was a writer, and maybe the most persistent.

Behind our grandparents' garden, Evans and I could see a wooded mountain, where, just a few months before his death, Bobby had found a marble he'd lost as a child. In my mind, Bobby was like the God of the Psalms, to whom a thousand years are like a day. My brother-in-law Travis tells the story of a time they were fishing together, back in 2014, and Bobby pointed out a rock in the middle of the creek.

"I was standing on that rock when I caught the prettiest rainbow trout. It weighed three and a half pounds. I had to fight it for ten minutes." Bobby went on to describe the test of the line and the bait he used.

Travis said, "When was that? Last week?"

Bobby said, in his usual slow, matter-of-fact way, "No, that was in the spring of 1947."

I tried to fish with Bobby once as a child. I was enthusiastic about the trip until Bobby pulled the first brim out of the water. The sight of its thrashing, bloody body tore my heart open, and I ran crying toward my mom. It was similar to the reaction Evans had when Bobby took him to help clean a deer he had killed. As Mom tells the story, Evans returned from the mountain with his face white and sad.

"He'll never be a hunter," Bobby said. "But that's okay." I never heard Bobby express tenderness toward animals, but he seemed to understand it. When I became a vegetarian, Mom worried that I'd offend him by not eating his venison, but Bobby approved of my choice as "healthy."

The thought of fishing still makes me sad, but I have always been secretly content that other members of my family have no compunction against it, because that was a way for them to bond with Bobby. The fishing contingent of our clan always came back from day trips with an air of returning from a longer adventure, relaxed and in high spirits and seeming to have a secret between them. Evans has memories of fishing with Bobby that span from his childhood to adulthood, and I was sure they were on his mind now.

"And then what happened?" Evans said, apropos of nothing, a little sorrow in his laugh. I smiled but was at a loss for what to say back to him. Perhaps that was fitting. "And then what happened?" was Bobby's catchphrase, one that always stumped me.

"Hello," I would say, answering the phone at my parents' house as a child.

"And then what happened?" Bobby would say, and I would have no idea how to respond.

I'm not a person who is often at a loss for what to say, but I was usually at a loss for what to say to Bobby. It felt like he sabotaged every attempt I made at finding common ground. We both liked to read, so I gave him books and inscribed them thoughtfully. He never read them. Once, he shuffled cards and told me a poker-story from his army days. I told him I loved cards, and asked if he'd teach me how to play poker. He said No: poker was sinful. I said we didn't have to play with money. Still, No.

Eventually, I ran out of material. Perhaps he gave up on me too, for near the end, he quit trying to give me a history lecture on World War II every time we were together. One of my final memories of Bobby—on a visit I made just a few months before he died— is of us sitting on his sofa and holding hands in silence.

More than anything, I wish Bobby and MeMe had spent their money—which they made through good stock investments and many years of extreme frugality—on themselves. My family would encourage them to get a house or cabin of their own, but they never did. "Your mother comes from a line of long-lived women," Bobby would say to my mom. "I want her to be taken care of when I'm gone." Sometimes my grandparents went without things they needed, senselessly. My sister bought my grandparents a car, once, when she deemed the one they had too dangerous to drive. Bobby appreciated it, but hinted that he would have preferred Shayna invest in some property he had his eye on.

There was a part of me that was frustrated with Bobby for all the effort and money he'd poured into the land at the end of his life. If he'd wanted to do something for his grandchildren, couldn't he have asked us what it was he'd wanted? Couldn't he have looked at and listened to our lives and guessed it wasn't that? The main gifts I wanted from him are the qualities I seek in other relationships: respect, emotional intimacy. But if Bobby was going to show his love with money, he might have put that money toward time together. Or he might have seen that four out of five of us grandchildren could have used money on hand: not for luxury, but to relieve real pressing need and anxiety. At the least, he could have simply refrained from buying that land, saved us from responsibility.

I was surprised at how much Bobby's death shook me. Standing with my brother that night, I felt like a visitor in a place where I had always taken my belonging for granted. One of my ties to this land was gone, and so I felt I belonged to it, and even to the Earth, a little less. I felt this in my body—a physical lightness that made me aware of my mortality in a way I hadn't been before.

■ ■ ■

MeMe periodically tells me that she wants Psalm 90:10 read at her funeral. *The length of our days is seventy years—or eighty, if we have the strength; yet their span is but trouble, and sorrow, for they quickly pass, and we fly away.* MeMe's life has been fraught with trouble and sorrow: from her hungry childhood, when her mother would step back from the table after a bite or two so her children could eat, to her teenage years when she was thrown out of her house after telling her mother she was pregnant, to her adulthood, when she cared for her mother in her old age and watched as most of her siblings and all of her children (with the exception of my mom) were pulled into a vortex of drugs, alcohol, paranoia, dysfunction, and despair. When she was young, MeMe would look at the magazines and think about how her life was going to be different than what she saw around her.

Now, she won't leave the mountains, or even her crumbling trailer, because it is where she feels close to Bobby. That means that her old age has offered her no respite from the tragedies of her family and community, which keep unfolding. In recent years, her niece's husband hanged himself about a mile from where MeMe lives, and the drug-dependent niece was arrested for trapping and mistreating her mother in the worst case of elderly abuse on file in North Carolina. That niece's sister, Carly, calls MeMe every few months asking for help with a bill, and MeMe tells her to come on down, she's happy to help. MeMe says she doesn't mind helping because Carly is trying. Carly's son has stolen ginseng from MeMe's property on multiple occasions, and has served jail time after MeMe reported him. I have heard MeMe on the phone arranging a court date regarding that great-nephew just moments after she's been on the phone with his mother, saying, "I can help with that. I'll be around all day today. See you then. I love you too."

Once, we passed by Carly's house on the way home from an errand, and I wondered if the thin young man climbing out of the car in her yard, wearing a ball cap and a frown, could be the cousin of mine who had caused so much trouble.

"There's the thief," MeMe said, as one might point out their local hardware store.

I always latched on to the "trouble and sorrow" part of that Bible verse because I assumed those were the words that resonated with MeMe. But after Bobby died, I found myself thinking *and we fly away*. I wondered if MeMe had felt this way as she had seen so many of her people and now her husband go: as if gravity was loosening its hold her, as though she could almost float, as though flying away would become inevitable.

■ ■ ■

At Bobby's funeral, the preacher read from the first chapter of Genesis:

"And God said, 'Let the water teem with living creatures, and let birds fly above the earth across the vault of the sky... Let the lands produce living creatures according to their kinds: the livestock, the creatures that move along the ground, and the wild animals.'" My sister, often composed to the point of seeming stern, stood up after the reading with her lips trembling. Then she gave a perfect speech. She'd recently been to an environmentalists' conference where everyone was asked to reflect on, then share, their most profound moment in nature. Her fellow attendees spoke of visiting national parks, camping in Patagonia, sailing remote parts of the earth. My sister said her most profound experience in nature had been walking through the woods with her grandfather—seeing the connection he had with the land after over eighty years spent on it, hearing bits of what he'd learned from decades of watching closely.

Once, she told us, they came across a dead tree lying on their path. Bobby taught my sister how trees continue to give to the land after they die, putting nutrients in the soil, providing food and haven for creatures. Shayna told us that Bobby's death was a little like that, for we would continue to benefit from the lessons he'd given and the life he had led.

Then the preacher spoke with an enormous amount of warmth—about the time Bobby had taken him on a treacherous hike deep into the woods, with no apparent purpose except the promise of a "picnic lunch," which turned out to not to be

MeMe's cooking, but ramps and sardines. We hadn't finished laughing about that before he told us about the time Bobby had called him and said, "Bert's just made one of her apple stack cakes. She'll be gone this week, so you should come over every night and eat a little with me." The preacher came over immediately, and Bobby pulled the cake out of the refrigerator only to drop the whole thing on the floor. He literally cried before deciding they should pick it up and eat it anyway.

At my mother's request, the preacher also noted that Bobby was "an environmentalist before being green was cool." I doubted that being green was cool yet in this rural Baptist church, in a county where Trump-Pence signs littered the otherwise gorgeous roadsides. I wasn't sure, though, for both the church and community surprised me in the aftermath of Bobby's death, in the best ways. There was a woman in her

Are all these nice people going to vote for Trump? *I kept wondering. I answered myself: Probably...so does that mean they're not actually nice? It was like a koan...*

forties, named Jackie, who kept us fed that week, and came over every day to help with whatever needed doing. Her sons came home from college to be at Bobby's funeral, which was incredibly moving to me, and even more-so when I saw how sad they genuinely were.

Are all these nice people going to vote for Trump? I kept wondering. I answered myself: *Probably...so, does that mean they're not actually nice?* It was like a koan: I couldn't shake a sense of the question's significance, but it was a puzzle without a solution. The people of the area display so many qualities I deeply respect and strive, but struggle, to enact in my own life. They express a depth of warmth and kindness with strangers that most of us save for our friends. They have the peace and patience to simply sit and "be" as well as to do, and a seemingly unwavering attention to the joys and needs of the present moment. Admiring the people of Bakersville as I do, my instinct is to blame the politics of the region on something outside of their control: a lack of education, perhaps? But maybe that would be patronizing. I never read *Hillbilly Elegy*, but Mom did because I gave it to her. She hated it (before hating it was cool). God save me from sounding like J.D. Vance.

MeMe said, when she learned Jackie's sons were coming to the funeral, "Those boys took Bobby on a fishing trip with some of their friends last summer and when he came back, he had a big old smile on his face and said it was about the most fun he'd ever had. He said those boys were climbing trees and jumping in the water and all sorts of things." I talked about the same trip to one of those boys—Colton—later. Colton was about eight-feet tall and gigantic all-around, including his lion's mane of red hair.

He stood next to me at dusk and said with fervor, "I loved your grandfather. My friends loved him too." He caught my eyes, clapped his hands together, then looked at the sky and said softly, "We'll miss him so much." He said it in the same tone that many people used that week when talking to me, including the preacher, as he'd whispered to me that he wasn't supposed to have favorite parishioners, but he just couldn't help it with Bob. They spoke as if their affection for and understanding of Bobby, though great, must be only a window into my own. Meanwhile, I lapped their stories up like a thirsty dog, for I was the one in need of a window.

■ ■ ■

After the funeral service, we went across the street to the cemetery, and Bobby was given the given the military burial he'd wanted. My sweet nephew, Jase, who was about eight at the time, gasped and jumped in my lap when they shot the first round of blanks, and I squeezed his thin, trembling body a little closer to mine. Past the soldiers shooting blanks, I could see the marble statue of Jesus I'd played under as a kid.

Every year, my family had come here in June for the Appalachian tradition of Decoration, a day when you and your children come back from wherever you've been scattered to picnic with your family and lay flowers on the graves at your home cemetery. Mom remembers both of her grandmothers being giddily excited when Decoration came around. They were some of the ones who hadn't scattered. Excited for the homecomings of old friends and old flames, they'd have new dresses ready weeks ahead of time. Mom always feels the need to explain the mountain ways to me. She's heard outsiders to the area say condescending things about mountain folks. She's always done her best to make sure I don't think of her homeland and the people she grew up around as backwards.

Specifically, she'd say she hoped I didn't think of Decoration as "morbid." I never did. Decoration felt like Easter. I loved everything about it: the potato salad and the smell of fresh-cut grass and lilies, the trouble my great-aunt Berm and Mom went to as they arranged the flowers, even the ones they were putting on the graves of strangers, the way Berm's granddaughter Brittany and I wandered aimlessly from one headstone to another, pausing with the butterflies, or rolled down the cemetery's hill for hours, because no one was in anything resembling a hurry.

On the day of Bobby's funeral, Brittany had to scurry back to Tennessee. Her toddler needed a nap.

"He's gettin' fussy," she said, heaving her son up on her hip with one arm and hugging me with the other. We'd barely gotten to talk.

But I spoke to other relatives I hadn't met before.

One of Bobby's nephews—not the bad one, I hoped—introduced himself to me. Laughing, he told me about a time when he and his cousins had gone on a several-day hunting trip with Bobby. On the last morning, they woke up early, eager to go home. Bobby hadn't had the success on that trip he had wanted to, and told his nephews he was going to go for one more quick ramble while they packed up camp. Hours passed, and at first the nephews were angry. Then they were worried. They thought he'd been killed.

"He wasn't in trouble," I said, thinking of how stubborn and single-minded Bobby had been. If he'd gone into the woods for venison, he wouldn't have emerged without it.

"Right," the nephew said. "And at last, we saw him coming over the hill with a huge buck on his shoulders. I'm talkin' massive. We were all mad at him for a second. But when we heard how far he'd lugged that thing, we laughed our asses off."

I laughed too. Bobby was a small man. His strength and dexterity, especially in his old age, shocked everybody. In 2013, I took my boyfriend (now husband) Dan to meet Bobby for the first time. Dan gasped when he saw Bobby start to climb the log steps of the Roan Mountain State Park alone. He ran up behind Bobby and took his arm.

By the time of our last walk with Bobby—about a month before his death—Dan knew better. My parents, my brother, Dan and I fell behind Bobby and let him lead the way, hiking up the steep mountains of his property, clearing wild tangles of trees and brush to make paths where there were none, finding his way back to where he'd started when the rest of us were lost.

I cherish the thought of both of those days with Bobby, especially the walk on the Roan. As we hiked, Bobby told Dan his favorite memory of me. I was a little girl, and the two of us were hiking with Mom on that very mountain. I remember it—the open sky, the way the sunshine and the breeze rippled between us and through the flame azaleas, giving motion to their splendid color. It seemed the mountain had no end. I kept running up and down the path, breathing in the smells of wet logs, iron, blossoms and mountain mud, feasting my eyes, and reveling in the spaciousness of it all.

"This must be what heaven feels like," I said again and again. I meant it. And even though I was only seven, I remember being surprised at myself for saying that, for being capable of feeling such ecstasy there. Before, when I'd imagined heaven, I'd always seen the ocean, dreamt of being near it, or better yet, in it, forever. Having grown up in South Carolina's lowcountry, salt water was all things to me: mystery and magic, source of healing, inspiration, and fun.

Mom always lamented that her three children loved the sea more than the mountains. It was one of the many things she felt she'd conceded by raising us where her husband was born instead of where she was born: the possibility that we even could feel her connection to Appalachia. But I've gotten glimpses of how she feels: on that day when I was seven, and again at Bobby's funeral. I can recall those days with visceral clarity, and feel in my body the unique ways my life could be rich and full, if I chose to live in North Carolina.

Science tells me that all of us are connected to each other, but I think I would feel it more, if I was always running into family or someone who knew my family. Faith tells me that I belong to this earth, but I'd know it better if I walked in the woods more, and stopped to drink the good water from the creek. If I lived in those mountains, I'd have autumn leaves and apple orchards. I'd have snow at Christmas, and the fearful-cold Toe River on hot summer days. If I lived in those mountains, I'd learn to play the fiddle, or either I'd dance to fiddle music every chance I got. To say *No* to something is not to be blind to its worth.

The summer after Bobby died, I moved to San Antonio, Texas to be with Dan. It was where he'd started his career, and for the time, he was tied there. We got engaged, then married. I taught fifth-and-sixth graders for a bit, and found myself ill-suited for it. Dan looked for new work, and was offered a remote job. That was our chance. We could go anywhere we wanted.

In the summer of 2018, we moved to San Diego.

■ ■ ■

"I don't know why none of my children have any interest in the land," Mom said mournfully on a car ride. This was in the summer of 2019, on a visit to my parents in South Carolina. On that car ride with my parents, the topic of discussion was that none of the grandchildren had so much as made a move to build a vacation home in the mountains, an interesting expectation to put on Dan and me, given that we don't own a primary home.

"You say that like attachment to the land is a moral virtue," I said.

"I was raised to believe it is," Mom said. "When *Gone with the Wind* came out, Daddy took me to the movies because he wanted me to see that scene." I knew which scene she was talking about: the one where Gerald O'Hara admonishes his daughter and sets her up for twelve years of misplaced gumption. When I watched the movie as a kid and as a teen, Mom would pause her house chores to rush into the room when it came on.

Do you mean to tell me, Katie Scarlett O'Hara,
that Tara, that land doesn't mean anything to
you? Why, land is the only thing in the world
worth workin' for, worth fightin' for, worth dyin'
for, because it's the only thing that lasts....And,
to anyone with a drop of Irish blood in them,
the land they live on is like their mother....It will
come to you, this love of the land.

"I know, I know," I said. "And that quote is just gut-wrenching, disgusting, and frankly ludicrous in context of a story where people are fighting and dying to stop the torture and enslavement of fellow humans."

I first read *Gone with the Wind* when I was eight. When my sister and brother had Black friends over to the house, Mom would tell me not to read the book in front of them. Beyond that, she and Dad never talked to me about anything that was wrong with the story. Even as a third-grader, though, I should have seen the problems better than I did: Rhett killing a Black man as a minor plot point in which he's represented as a chivalrous rascal; Ashley casually joining the KKK; Rhett raping and impregnating Scarlett in an iconic scene that's supposed to be sexy; the way us readers are made to feel as though Scarlett screwed up their love, when Rhett was the one that hit her with enough force to knock her down a flight of stairs.

On that car ride, Mom sighed as though it was a real disappointment to have such a block-headed daughter, one who can only see things as black-and-white.

"I suppose it's a generational thing," she said.

Perhaps I should have stepped in then and told her what our land means to me. But I latched on to the dig at my generation, mainly because it was nonsensical. In my travels, I have met many people my mom's age who have been wanderers all their lives and are proud of it, as though it is proof that their courageous, lotus blossom souls can bloom in whatever mud they're planted. I secretly roll my eyes at them: I'm a wanderer, too, by choice, and might always be, but it's stupid to act superior about it. Wandering is just a choice to go wide instead of deep.

"Hey now," I said. "Dan's parents are your age, and neither of them lives in the town they grew up in." Like her father might have done, Mom ignored me.

"Young people these days just don't have the connection to the land that we do," she said. "Explain it to her, Doug."

Dad, who lives in a home that has been in his family for 250 years, thought very hard before he said, with force behind each word, "It's like your identity is tied up in the land. You're connected when you're walking in a place all your people have

I secretly roll my eyes at them: I'm a wanderer, too, by choice, and might always be, but it's stupid too act superior about it. Wandering is just a choice to go wide instead of deep.

walked, and your ancestors have lived. And if you choose to leave that place, it's like you're losing yourself."

When I spoke again, though, I genuinely wasn't meaning to contradict Dad, whose point I had taken. I suppose I was just trying to show that my temporary choices also came from a soulful rather than shallow place.

I said, "When I travel, I feel more and more a part of the big picture, more a part of everything that is. That makes me feel profoundly connected."

"That's two different things," Dad said.

"Sure," I said. "It's two different sentiments, but you can make room for both. Augustine said the world is a book, and those who do not travel read only one page."

"And Faulkner said his own postage stamp of native soil was worth writing about and that he would never live long enough to exhaust it," Dad said. I might have said that even Faulkner made it out to California, to try his hand at screenwriting, and though he referred to Los Angeles as "the plastic asshole of the world," he was also intensely critical of the South. But Dad's tone was hurt.

"I'm not saying that Early Branch or any other place is lacking interest or richness," I said. I'm saying every place has its own qualities that are worth 'writing about' or at least experiencing."

"I guess I didn't explain it well enough," Dad said. He seemed sad and frustrated, and I didn't know what to say. I couldn't promise him I'd ever move back. I had fallen in love with a man whose pride in the cool caves and scorching deserts of South Texas mirrored the attachment I felt to South Carolina's marshlands and Spanish moss. I'd grown fond of Texas while I lived there, but I never loved it, and I doubted that Dan could come to love South Carolina or North Carolina in the way I did. It was better, I figured, to live in a place we were both drawn to.

On the other hand, I wasn't sure my journey would feel complete if all that swimming downstream didn't take me back to Carolina. I realized that, actually, in Texas, on a camping trip with friends. It was a cold night, and we were sitting by the river, passing a flashlight around and reading poetry aloud. Our friend Joe introduced one poem by saying its writer had spent years traveling from place to place looking to live somewhere suitable to his health. Finally, he'd given up on his pursuit, and settled in Samoa, where he wrote the words that would go on his tombstone.

Nothing would do but to share that poem with my parents. I read it aloud to them right before I moved to California. In doing so, I thought I was expressing what I felt too vulnerable to say directly: *I hope I'll come back one day, for good.* My voice cracked and I started weeping as I read the second stanza.

> *This be the verse you grave for me:*
> *Here he lies where he longed to be.*
> *Home is the sailor, home from the sea*
> *And the hunter home from the hill.*

"Robert Louis Stevenson," my dad said, sounding bored.

"We know that poem," Mom said, in a tone that suggested there was nothing special about it. My parents both looked at me inquisitively for a moment. Their faces seemed to ask what all the fuss was about. In the end, they decided the answer was nothing, and looked away.

■ ■ ■

After Bobby's burial, my brother-in-law scanned the ground for blanks and tucked them into his pocket. Later that week, he dropped them in one of the rivers Bobby had fished at as a child and later as an old man, with Travis and Jase. I went too, and my desire to do that surprised me, since I have always associated fishing and guns with needless violence. Perhaps I just wanted to connect with Bobby and his memory in any way I could.

Or perhaps I was able that day to connect with Bobby in a way I hadn't before—to ponder his views on fishing and hunting (take what you need from the earth; nourish yourself, but be reverent about it and don't waste a thing), to reflect on the military burial and Bobby's pride in his service, which he must have viewed as a mark of courage and loyalty, and to not hide from myself how many things about the Lily Branch Baptist Church I like: its gray stone walls and the spacious feeling the high rafters give the small chapel; the simple, unpretentious approach to spirituality; the way the church ladies made a feast for the family and served it to us before the service; the way the preacher had spent hours of leisure at Bobby's side.

It's not that I was ignorant before of Bobby's views on politics, on guns, on eating animals, or that I changed my own after he was gone. Rather, after he went, I was better able to accept his feelings with equanimity instead of pushing them from my mind, trying to form a distance between my views and the ones of my family.

To Bobby, *socialism* was a dirty word—but it is leaning into that word that has helped me make peace with his memory, to see him as one of the ones I'm fighting for, and not against. I can hardly imagine a person more different from me than Bobby, and yet the world I imagine is one that would treat him better than the one in which he grew up: one in which neither he nor his family would ever have scrambled for survival, one in which he might have been nurtured in spirit as well as body, one in which his love of learning and sharing knowledge might have flourished.

I don't know what I am going to do with the mountain land that comes to me. Selling the land for profit seems wrong, but so does hoarding it. I've thought about founding a refugee camp, or perhaps a retreat for artists and writers. Lately, it has occurred to me that perhaps I have a responsibility to give the land back to the descendants of displaced Cherokee people. If I shared these plans with Mom or MeMe, they might see them as a betrayal, if only because all of those options are far from what Bobby or they would have envisioned. In their minds, the love of our land hasn't come to me yet.

■ ■ ■

Dan and I vacationed in the Grand Tetons in July of 2019. I had an appreciation for the white, jagged mountains there, and the pines that dotted them, but the feeling of awe everyone else expressed evaded me. When we visited MeMe a few weeks later that August, though, I felt that same deep sense of reverence and amazement that I had as a little girl for the beauty on the Roan. I felt full that week—inexpressibly happy, almost at peace.

It reminded me of being eight years old. Then, a two-week summer trip to the mountains came to a close, and I found that I couldn't stand the thought of leaving MeMe. So, Mom and Dad went home and I stayed another month or so.

MeMe asked me, apparently, what I wanted to do during the visit, and she swears I responded, "Something with stitchery." However it came about, she made an incredible quilt, while I looked over her shoulder and played with thimbles and pieces of fabric. I have the quilt still. It has a row representing each of the grandchildren and our interests at the time. (My row has doll clothes, a cat, and a book.) When we weren't at her sewing machine or the Mountain Piecemakers Quilt Guild, MeMe and I were in her kitchen making biscuits and jam and chocolate meringue, cracking open dusty jars of spicy tomato juice she'd put away, or on the porch, keeping company with the fireflies, unzipping and breaking green beans into a pail. We'd stay up late at night, watching *Gilligan's Island* and *Three's Company*, which she seemed to find as hilarious as I did, except when there was a raunchy scene.

MeMe doesn't have the energy for most of those things anymore, and *Nick at Nite* isn't what it used to be. But what I've always loved most about time with MeMe is the conversation. She has a fresh, pithy take on everything, and an offbeat sense of humor.

During that 2019 visit, while I choked on a large piece of watermelon, MeMe looked on with her arms crossed and said, in a tone that conveyed equal parts shock, pity and disapproval, "Why, it put the whole thing in its mouth!"

"Huh! I wonder why it did that," Dan said. He crossed his arms too, and nearly died laughing.

"I don't know," MeMe said, as I put one of the regurgitated pieces of melon back in my mouth and chewed it up. "It must not be very smart."

When this greatness passes from the Earth, I will miss her terribly. I can already anticipate the things I may do to feel closer to her: perhaps I'll try my hand at growing food and flowers; maybe I'll learn to can or find some small way to take up the art of stitchery. I'll hang up her drawings in my home. But I know I'll feel nearest to her when I go to the mountains, and that is something I'll do again and again, as long as I'm alive.

When I was a child, I felt like I had a place in the mountains of North Carolina, but after that 2019 trip I began to think they had a place in me. That feeling had grown in me like a seed for a few years, and seemed to ripen that summer. It seemed I finally had the devotion to the area that Bobby always wanted me to have, a joyful love that turned out to be a natural extension—or dimension—of myself.

Those Blue Ridge mountains are often purple up close, and being old and worn down, they have a softer look to them than the mountains of the west. The trees have my attention now: the beeches with their pale, scarred trunks, the sugar maples whose intricate leaves become yellow and spotted in autumn, smelling of wet earth, but staying sturdy under my feet; the modest buckeyes, and the dogwoods, whose tiny, perfect blossoms make me think of dryads, the convergence of another world with our own.

And of course, there are the massive Carolina Hemlocks. Those are the ones that line and shelter the wooded path that leads to a local swimming hole and throw dark shadows on the water. I love how the trees in the area crowd up against each other and overlap their branches. They make for a sense of impenetrable mystery, tangled as they are with moss and fern. I wonder if these trees will one day exert the same pull on me the ocean does—an aching feeling when I am away. I wonder if the sadness I feel now, when I leave, shows me they already do. ■

HALF ODE TO THE ROPE SWING I NEVER CLIMBED

There is a length of old rope tied to an elm on the bank of
Fishing Creek that I used to pass on drives with my family.
Plenty of kids jumped from it, but I was never invited to go to
Fishing Creek or the dollop of earth in the middle nicknamed
The Beach. Even if I had been invited, I would not have gone.
I knew from science camp how thick that water was with
crayfish, tadpoles, and countless larvae like cyborgs in their
brown armor, antennae, and needling legs. Even if I had been
invited, I would not have jumped. The only brown kid on the
bank, too worried about a graceless descent into the mud,
chalky feet calloused from ballet, arms crossed to protect
breasts that took too long to arrive. Though I never tried the
swing, I admired that someone with a ladder and great care
knotted it thrice at the base to support your feet as you swung.
I picture myself there, greening rope in hand. I am fragile like
the mayfly hatchling with no love for stagnant pools. I look to
the sun who knows that when it matters, I will choose flight.

RITA MOOKERJEE

A SNAKE HEART CAN SLIDE UP AND DOWN THE LENGTH OF ITS BODY

a golden shovel after Aimee Nezhukumatathil

Perhaps this is why I often look at ease. My snake-
skin picks up on any given vibe then tells my heart
where to go.   In this way, I can

always work a room. It is not possible to slide
under my skin. I have no under. I am built up
of earthen lace   part of an infinite body.

My heart bounces through rings of bone, down
my pronged ribs and back up the brief length of
me   like the top   of a carnival game its

bulb screaming then gone.   As a snake, my body
is always ready. It is not possible to stab my heart;
                    that thing is always on the move.

RITA MOOKERJEE

ORIGINS OF VANITY

Djinn usually go for oil lamps, but this was
a vintage perfume bottle: the old Hollywood
kind with an atomizer and a silky cream tassel.
The bottle was frosted and broad shouldered.

It presided over the dresser like a queen. Though
there was no liquid inside, I could still smell light
bursts of sweetness in the spritzed air: puff
of talc, rosehip, and magnolia. So nostalgic

that I might have imagined it. When my mom
went to the store, I'd anoint myself with
the not-perfume and muse that I too might
have small treasures like these of my own.

That bottle was who I wanted to be: adorned
and adored. One day the pale glass slipped
from my hand and hit the dresser with a crack.
Only the top corner was broken, but really

the bottle was ruined. Now it could never
house a chypre or a jasmine musk or me. My
mom sighed, *who told you to touch that?* I did
not answer, but she knew I was thirsty for beauty

and excess, that my home is at their nexus.
Later this impulse would darken, turning me
into someone who lives purely for indulgence.
Luxe or bust. This is my earliest memory of her.

RITA MOOKERJEE

EVERYONE LIVING THE DREAM

LEAH BRENNAN RENBERG

Every afternoon at about 3:15, Elsie Hamlet picked one task to complete: return an email to a parent, grade one essay or a few quizzes. The students had been dismissed. They were riding the bus or at sports practice or play rehearsal, and the hallway noise, the slamming of metal lockers, the laughing, shouting, screeching, running of teenagers, almost constant from 7:00 to 3:00, had finally faded away, leaving only the sound of the clock.

She turned off the overhead lights and flipped through Opal's reading journal, a pink spiral notebook with ENGLISH written across the cover in letters that looked like they'd been painstakingly stenciled. Elsie skimmed the contents. In the margins, with an erasable green pen, she added a little note or a check mark here and there, one comment per page. She was doing the thing that she hoped just meant she was tired, combining words into nonsense: *Thisn't. Cadd more detail?* Her erasing left the pages a dingey brown, which Opal would probably find disruptive to her mental state.

Opal was not a very good writer, but she tried hard and thought that meant she should receive an A. She longed for the A, coveted it. Elsie dreaded returning work to students like Opal. She sometimes held on to essays and quizzes for weeks because she knew what was coming.

Elsie was not a new teacher, but she sometimes acted like one. She sometimes let them get to her. That day, she'd gone too far.

It was the period after lunch. Opal received her essay on *Pride and Prejudice* with trembling hands. Elsie had given her a B+. The analysis was weak, and she used the same examples used by every student who had ever consulted the internet: Elizabeth walking miles to see poor, sick Jane. Lydia buying an ugly bonnet. If Opal had asked for help, Elsie could have guided her to a better thesis. The B+ was a gift, but Elsie could never say that to a student. There was so much she couldn't say.

Opal whimpered. Ms. Hamlet just didn't understand—her parents would kill her! Roughly half of Elsie's students had parents who would *literally* kill them if they didn't get an A.

Opal was seriously going to die. A few others joined in Opal's chorus: they were all going to die! They, too, had earned

B+s. One of them had earned an A-. The kids who earned Cs worked quietly at their desks.

Elsie took a deep breath, steadied her face, and crouched down in front of Opal's desk. "Do you want to take a break? Go to the nurse's office?" Opal practically lived in the nurse's office. Once she was gone, Elsie could circulate in peace, pretending to examine her students' work, doling out praise until she could dismiss them and finally be able to use the bathroom.

But then after class, Opal returned to gather her belongings and go over what she had missed. Like Elsie had all the time in the world and hadn't had to pee for three hours. The other students had left, and it was just the two of them. In the room next door, Val, the ninth-grade English teacher, was playing a film version of *Lord of the Flies*. The sound of drumming was coming through the wall. Opal sat obediently at her desk, expecting instruction. Elsie sat down at the desk next to Opal's. Its surface, marred by ink and pencil, appeared older than the school itself.

"Sometimes," Elsie said. "The other students just want to slap you in the face."

■ ■ ■

Opal played the harp, of all things for a teenager to play. A stuffed animal the size and shape of a softball was clipped to the zipper of her backpack, a rat or maybe a sloth, the kids were obsessed with sloths. She was on the track team and ran the longest distances. Elsie was forty and had a basket of dirty laundry in her trunk, which she intended to wash in her mother's washing machine and dry in her drier.

If the Opal told her parents what Elsie had said, or told another teacher, or told another student who then told their parents or a teacher, Elsie would have to participate in a series of long and uncomfortable meetings. She'd have to apologize. She could probably be fired, or disciplined in an embarrassing way, forced to resign, added to the list of child abusers.

Opal was widely admired because she made what appeared to be agonizing efforts to overcome her own pitifulness, like managing to sometimes hold in her tears at the dreaded B+ or when the fake gun shots rang out during an active shooter drill, when they all had to huddle against the wall farthest from the door and the windows.

But the other kids rolled their eyes—the other kids did want to slap her in the face, Elsie was sure of it, and when Elsie finally told her the truth, Opal, after a gasp, a moment of stunned silence, had laughed, a nervous laughter, and then she was nodding, as though in agreement, or at least a measure of understanding, as though Elsie had answered a question she'd been asking for a long time.

She gripped her stuffed sloth by its face, kind of squeezed it like a stress ball, and swung her mammoth fuchsia backpack over one shoulder. When she left, she quietly closed the door, trying not to make a sound, trying to make sure that her efforts would be noticed, the slowest door-closing Elsie had ever witnessed. It felt like hours.

Elsie longed to drape herself in her jacket and leave the scene of her crime. She'd never said those words aloud, but now she realized that deep in the dark cavity that was her brain, a little tape recorder had been playing in her ear for years, daring her to crush someone as she'd been crushed, when her diving coach had said the very same thing to her, when she was suffering from panic attacks, exiting the pool ungracefully, heaving, beaching herself on the deck. *The other kids just want to slap you in the face.* And now she'd finally done it.

What would it be like to be fired? She had one backup plan, but it wasn't practical in terms of a salary or health insurance. Her YA novel-in-progress, 120 pages that her college professor, whom she had emailed and begged to please give at least the first chapter a read, had said included *all the elements of a story*. He advised her to submit it. Every Sunday, she chose another agent to send her materials. Her cover letter was exactly one page and full of quirky but relevant details about her qualifications and knowledge, about her plot and themes and main character, who was unbelievable at gymnastics, unbelievable at math, a real role model. Someone young readers would want to be friends with.

The bell was ringing. At her desk, Elsie hid behind her laptop screen and stuck her hands up her shirt to warm them. The heat wouldn't be turned on until November. The gray sky

A skin had formed at the top of her room-temperature coffee, and it broke apart as she swirled her mug like it was wine. She sucked it down...

meant that no afternoon sun would be streaming through the broken blinds hanging crookedly over the window. A dozen texts had arrived from her mother. She signed them all *Love, Mom.* A skin had formed at the top of her room-temperature coffee, and it broke apart as she swirled her mug like it was wine. She sucked it down, scrolling in a mindless but focused way that made her feel like she was a little bit high, like the rest of the world had dissolved into the air, and she was safe and alone inside a small, quiet room.

Someone was knocking. Elsie let go of her nice warm boob and pretended to be engrossed in her work.

"Yoo-hoo! It's me!"

"Hey, Val."

"I wanted to pop in and say hello. We've been two ships passing in the night today! I heard you were out yesterday?"

Was it only yesterday that she'd stayed home? "Just a bad cold."

"My kids came down with something, one of those forty-eight hour bugs? It's going around! Maybe you had what my kids have? Runny nose?" Val carefully, silently mouthed the word *diarrhea.*

"For sure. That must've been it." In the search bar, she typed every swear word.

"I just wanted to say a quick hi and goodbye!"

Elsie managed to say hi and goodbye without screaming at the top of her lungs.

Getting back to her screen, she scrolled past an ad for leggings, a cell phone video of a devastating flood in a country she couldn't recognize. Then some grainy black and white footage of women doing gymnastics in the fifties, little leaps and twirls even she could do. Could she have gone to the Olympics if she were living in the fifties? Won a medal for lifting her leg into a shaky arabesque, cartwheeling in a slow dismount? She scrolled faster, paused on a starving dog being fattened up and healed at an animal rescue. He took his first shaky steps in a fenced-in dirt patch. Elsie was crying. She'd been holding her bladder for so long she no longer had to go.

She was out of coffee and low on water, but the thought of leaving her classroom filled her with an immense dread. Ignoring her thirst, she clicked on the ad for Satin Rich Flame Shine with Moisturizer, then a long-wear mascara, bamboo brushes, an eye shadow palette with forty different colors, she kept going, then returned to the beginning. She added the Satin Rich Flame Shine with Moisturizer to her cart.

Another text from her mother. *I spoke with the lawyer. Please call. Love, Mom.* Why was her mom speaking to a lawyer? Her parents had been divorced for more than twenty-five years. But her mother just couldn't stop trying to take care of Elsie's father, even though he'd left her for a woman still in college and since their breakup had probably about a dozen other girlfriends, Elsie could hardly keep track. The only one she remembered at all was the first one, Jessica, who wore tall boots and a black leather jacket and made Elsie's mom terribly angry. Jessica, for a couple of years, was a cool older sister who took Elsie to the mall and once gave her a very small bottle of vodka, the kind they keep in a basket by the register, so small they appear to be child-sized. But then one day, Jessica's leather jacket was missing from the hooks by the front door at her dad's apartment, and every other weekend became a chore of over-boiled spaghetti and sleeping in her least favorite T-shirts in a bed that did not feel like her own.

At 3:25, Elsie finished Opal's reading journal. B+. She checked her email. Every store she had ever shopped at wanted to give her a deal. The Democratic candidate needed her. She donated five dollars. And then, she saw it, halfway down the page, an email from an agent she was so sure would have loved her novel. From the sound of the rejection letter, the agent may not have read a single word. Or maybe she read one page, barfed, or laughed her head off but not in a good way.

She opened a new tab. There was a GoFundMe for an acquaintance from graduate school, whose daughter had leukemia. She donated twenty dollars. There was another post about her high school reunion, which was next Saturday. Kate Frey had RSVPed. So had Ira. So had Liam Jameson, and Taylor T., and Jessie.

She hesitated over the invitation to the reunion. Twenty years. Twenty years!

Fine.

She clicked "Yes."

■ ■ ■

Elsie would kill to be getting a B+ in literally anything she did. She mostly felt like a C+, or even a plain old D. She definitely got a D on laundry. D on cleaning the grime out of the sink drain. D on calling her dad. Who, according to her mom, really needed to hear from her right at this moment, not because of his poor health, or his rapidly accruing dementedness, but because his newest girlfriend had recently absconded with most of his savings. *Please call your father. He needs to hear how this all makes you feel. Love, Mom.*

A C+ on remembering to make herself a turkey sandwich nearly every day for lunch. Maybe a B on calling in sick when she was actually hung over only once or twice a year. No more than half a dozen. That was something.

At 3:35, she began to gather her things. Staying late, even by five minutes, was proof she was still okay. It was how she'd told herself she would know if she had a problem. If she couldn't at least stay a few extra minutes, just to finish up what she was working on, then it was time to admit she needed help. But so far, she'd been able to stay past 3:30 every day since the first day of school, back in August, which felt like five to ten years ago.

On the walk to her car, she checked her phone. Ira had liked her *yes* to the reunion. What a funny, brave thing for him to do, but that was Ira. Ira! She hadn't thought about him in what seemed like years, but then she remembered she had thought about him the last time she was at the grocery store, looking at the wall of beer, and noticing the stack of silver thirty packs. *Beer Mountain.*

Ira, with his fluffy brown dandelion hair, his navy blue and maroon striped rugby shirts and tan cargo pants, which she once borrowed after falling into the creek behind his house when they were in middle school. They'd been trying to catch a small frog to see if frogs always peed on your hand when you held them, which they had heard from someone at school.

"It's supposed to be some kind of defense mechanism," Elsie said. She lined up her sandals and left them in the leaves at the base of an oak tree that was split down the middle from lightening but was somehow still alive. The rocks along the edges of the creek were partially covered by the water, and she tried not to make a splash as she crossed them. "They think if they pee on you, you'll let them go."

"I'm not scared of a little frog pee." Ira had already made it across the creek, jumping from rock to rock.

"I'm definitely not scared." But as she crossed the rocks, following Ira's path, she slipped and lost her balance. One foot stepped into the freezing water, and the shock of it caused her to run towards the bank. The mud of the creek bed was slippery, and she went down again.

Letting a frog pee in her hand as she sat in her wet denim skirt was the moment she realized she had a best friend.

She left her wet sandals on Ira's front porch, afraid to bring them inside, even to the space he called a mud room. He gave her a pair of his sister's socks, put her skirt in the drier, and made hot chocolate in the microwave. Wearing Ira's soft, baggy clothes, his sister's warm, striped socks, she had never felt more comfortable in her life.

To Elsie, the vibe felt almost brotherly. By the time they got to high school, they were smoking the crumbly dry schwag Ira stole from his sister out of a soda can. Elsie had only recently quit her elite gymnastics team because her parents *didn't like what it was doing to her*, but really because after the divorce they couldn't afford it, and she had all the time in the world.

When they were high one afternoon, she told Ira she thought of him as a brother.

"Dude, no way."

"Way."

"I always thought it was like, sisterly. Because you kind of remind me of my sister."

"Oh."

But like, I also remind me of my sister? So like, we're sisters together, but we're also *one sister*. Together."

"Totally," she said. They were one sister. Together.

They watched hours of television, sometimes walked

They watched hours of television, sometimes walked twenty-five minutes to the corner store, where they could buy chips. It was the best time of Elsie's life.

twenty-five minutes to the corner store, where they could buy chips. It was the best time of Elsie's life.

College was by far the worst time. Within a month of her first year at Penn State, she had dropped out and was living at home. *Withdrawn*, her mother always corrected her. She had withdrawn from college for reasons that were medical and emotional. On the weekends, she worked the register at Denny's and sometimes helped the servers bus tables. She snuck fries from other people's plates when no one was watching.

At Harvard, Ira started dating a woman who had gone to a private school, who didn't like that he smoked pot, and who really didn't like that he used to smoke pot with Elsie, a girl who was such a close friend, what was that all about, the girlfriend just didn't get it. Ira revealed this all to Elsie on Instant Messenger over Thanksgiving break, like his hands were tied, like he was married to this woman and had been for years. *She doesn't like that you call me.*

She saw Ira the following summer, at someone's house, a basement she had never been in, she couldn't remember whose it was or even who else had been there that night, besides Ira. Everyone had finished their first year of college. They compared dorms and dining halls and homecomings and freshman seminars. Ira had broken up with the college girlfriend. Elsie remembered the dark basement. An old kitchen table and chairs. The pool table in the center. A couch along one side.

"I always liked you," Ira said. His hand was on her knee, squeezing it. They'd finished their game of pool, she couldn't remember how it ended, but Ira had pulled her down onto the couch in a bear hug. No one could really see them, although she could hear them laughing, playing quarters, the sound of a coin landing in a cup. They all seemed to be winning. The couch smelled faintly of cat pee, and when he kissed her, and she wished they were back in the creek catching frogs. She tried to move like she was supposed to be moving, tilting her head in the right direction at the right time. It was like watching herself perform in a play.

"We're like one sister," she said into his ear, instead of kissing him.

"What?"

"Nothing." She held her breath and tried not to make a sound as he bit her on the shoulder. They'd been drinking, but he was Ira, the person she loved most in the world.

But it didn't feel like love. The sound of coins bouncing on the table made her feel like she was in a casino, and Ira kept pulling her hair. He couldn't figure out her buttons, he couldn't figure out her bra, and she was glad when he gave up and asked if she wanted another beer.

When he finally brought her home, she asked him to pull over so she could throw up. The worst part was the way he had looked at her as she climbed back into the passenger seat, like he was finally seeing what his college ex-girlfriend had been seeing for months.

But that was almost twenty years ago. It was the last time she had seen him, or anyone from high school in real life.

She saw them all online, announcements of engagements and weddings and new houses and babies, all the staged photoshoots, happy couple in a pile of leaves, happy couple kissing or feeding each other cake, a tiny baby wearing a headband with an enormous flower on the side, like a second head. Some of her classmates had new last names, and a few of them she couldn't remember if they'd gone to high school together or if they'd met some other time and place. Ira went only by his first and middle name. Ira Edward. She liked his posts aggressively. A video he had taken of a cat, sunning itself luxuriously on a concrete stoop across the street from where he was standing. A brick house, colorful flowers in pots lining the front steps, and this cat, flat on its back, then wriggling around like it was doing a weird move in a floor routine, then stretching its limbs, its entire, fluffy body open to the sun. The caption, Goals.

She had liked his college graduation photo, his black robe barely hanging on his shoulders, the red tassel grazing his hair, which he had trimmed. She liked the photo album he was tagged in, of his wedding, on a beach.

Ira liking her RSVP felt like a warm embrace, like they were friends again. Her backpack felt lighter on her shoulders. Another teacher saw her leaving and yelled, Happy to be going home, I see! I'm right behind you! The teacher didn't seem to have any idea that Elsie had insulted a student. It seemed at least for now she was safe.

■ ■ ■

A week before the reunion, Opal played her harp at a school assembly. When she had volunteered during homeroom, she raised her hand shakily, and before she spoke, she put her head back down on the desk, then sat up again, then nearly slid from her chair to the floor. She guessed she could play a song? If no one else wanted to? She'd be lucky if she didn't have a meltdown!

"Great! I'll make a note of that." Elsie fanned herself with a paperback, waiting for it all to end.

Elsie couldn't be sure, she was unfamiliar with harp music, but the performance seemed to go well. Opal, straddling an enormous instrument, looked more confident than Elsie had ever seen her. With blue-polished nails, she plucked at the strings furiously but gently, her head tapping out the beat, which was quick and rigid. Her little white sneakers. The notes drifted from low to high and back again. Elsie was almost proud.

But honestly, it seemed difficult if not impossible to make a harp sound particularly offensive. It was a harp! And as the applause diminished, the sounds of the Opal's crying became loud and clear, and the orchestra teacher, Mr. Thomas, rushed to the stage to steady the harp as Opal eased herself from her stool and sort of cascaded down to the floor. What happened in homeroom had been a preview. The soccer coach and the school nurse escorted her slowly down the stairs, as though she'd been gravely injured. More applause. The nurse patted her on the back. So brave! Elsie very nearly went home early.

At home, laundry still in the trunk, she Googled *How to do a high school reunion.* Her laptop was hot to the touch, and the sound of the motor running reminded her of the sound of her dad's razor. He used to trim his beard almost every morning, shaping it, adjusting the angles around his chin, and she used to sit on the floor of the bathroom waiting for him to finish. One day, when she was about three years old, he shaved it. He was completely changed. Her parents told her she screamed when he tried to pick her up.

On the internet, she learned that she should try not to get wasted, that she should try not to stand off in the corner with a friend and gossip about everyone, that she should dress up but still be herself.

Her cart held thirty-eight items. Close to $800. One by one, she deleted what she knew she wouldn't use, like loose

On the internet, she learned that she should try not to get wasted, that she should try not to stand off in the corner with a friend and gossip about everyone, that she should dress up but still be herself.

powders and liquid eyeliner. All she really wanted was the bright red lipstick. It was probably made of plastic and the fat of endangered whales, but it was dressed up. It was not herself.

The night of the reunion, she tried on all three pairs of her jeans. She took a break and lay down on the couch, smoking half a joint and sipping a room-temperature whiskey, because the ice tray was empty. She graded one more reading journal. She'd had them for three weeks. At school, everything was quiet and normal, except that Opal tracked her even more diligently, as though Elsie was grading her on her ability not to break eye contact. She still refused to ask for help on her thesis statements.

In the rusted mirror above her sink, she applied her expensive lipstick, wiped it off, reapplied it. Inside her jewelry box, a moth had died next to an old mood ring, and when she tried to pick it up with a tissue, it disintegrated into the velvet. She tried on all her shirts. She didn't want to dress like a teacher, in her frumpy blouses and pilly cardigans. Her black turtleneck sweater made her look something like a writer. Dangly earrings seemed appropriate. High heels were too dangerous for a night of potentially ugly drinking, but she tried on every pair of flats, even though it was cold and late November, and she knew it might rain.

And it did rain. The parking lot at the restaurant where the reunion was being held was full. Rows of SUVs. She wondered if Ira had already arrived, or if he was running late. *Ira Time*, she remembered. He was probably on Ira Time.

Inside, she took a breath at the door to the event space in the back of the restaurant, the Tap Room, which was evidently not soundproofed. The rowdiness of forty-year-olds from the suburbs reminded her of the sound of movies and YouTube clips coming through the wall between her classroom and Val's. Loud enough to be disruptive, but not clear enough for Elsie to understand the words. With her knuckle, she blotted her lipstick. Her left foot was wet from the puddle she'd stepped in getting out of her car.

Excuse me, a server said, squeezing behind her. "This isn't a great place to, you know, hang out." The server practically had to shout because of the noise behind the door.

"Sorry, sorry," Elsie said. "I'm going to the reunion."

But the server had already moved on.

■ ■ ■

A tight circle of three couples stood nearly blocking the door, like they were deciding whether or not to leave. Three tall men with their arms around three women, diamonds big enough to be weaponized. Jessie! How are you? Jessie was pregnant! And Taylor T. was pregnant, too! And oh my god, Liam! It's so good to see you!

Hey. Buddy.

So, Liam didn't recognize her. Big deal. They'd hardly been friends, only teammates on the four- or five-member diving team that consistently placed too low to qualify for states.

Pushing past the group of couples, she searched for Ira. So many of the men had lost their hair, a few had gained an unhealthy amount of weight and looked as pregnant as Jessie and Taylor T. At a distance, the women looked the same as they did at eighteen. Kate Frey had four kids and still had the bearing of a super model.

Elsie squeezed herself through the crowd towards the bar, having the same conversation with everyone she passed. She learned everyone was doing well, up to the same-old, same-old, living the dream. They hadn't changed a bit. She met some spouses, but most people had come alone. The spouses were at home with the children. The kids. Everyone had kids.

Finally, she was at the bar, waiting her turn. The sound of the music and the voices made the air feel heavier. She adjusted her earring, freeing it from her hair. There was her squishy left foot. Her sweaty underboob, the turtleneck sweater a bad idea, the room at least seventy-five degrees. Her phone vibrating. *Have you called him? Love, Mom.* She checked her email, like she was popular, but all she had received was a rejection letter and a request for a one-week extension on a homework assignment from Opal.

She felt a tap on her shoulder.

"Ira!"

"It's me. It's Ira. Let's get you a drink."

And suddenly, the bartender appeared.

■ ■ ■

Soft brown hair, now a little shorter, neater, like it was being maintained. Different glasses, smaller frames. No more cargo pants, no more rugby shirt. Jeans and a pullover. His wife clung to his arm.

This was Sandra. Elsie recognized her from the wedding album, her cottony, simple dress, a hair-down-in-loose-curls, barefoot sort of ceremony. They had met on a study abroad trip. Sandra was drinking white wine with an ice cube. They were up to the same-old, same-old. Sandra worked at a textbook company as an editor.

"And what are you up to these days?" Ira said. "Living the dream?"

"For sure. Living the dream." She was practically shouting at them. "I've been working on something. A novel."

"You look like a writer!"

"I remember you did well in English."

"I was maybe a B+ in English."

"Do you have any agent?"

"I have, um, I've had some interest." Elsie took a long drink of a light beer, pacing herself, hoping one of them would start talking, but they both continued to stare at her. With her sleeve, she wiped the sweat from her hairline, but the wool caused static, and her hair was suddenly in her face, in her mouth. "I, you know, I sometimes feel like because I didn't go to Harvard, I'll never be taken seriously."

"Ira went to Harvard!"

"Well, it's not like I'm using my degree."

"It's true!" Sandra punched him in the arm. "He writes essays for this company? Students pay him to write their essays, basically. It's morally corrupt. But he's so good at it!" She punched him again, then kissed him on his sleeve. Elsie wondered if any of her students had benefitted from Ira's services, and for a second, she hated him and his business for making her job harder and more pointless.

"Dude. Else. You should use my degree. Here," he said, tapping her on each shoulder with his glass. "I dub you Harvard grad."

"I don't think it works that way."

"No, seriously. Just say your name is Ira Belman. It can be your pen name. I don't even use it anymore. Sandra and I put our names together and made a new one. I'm Ira Belrich now."

"We're the Belriches!"

"Our parents hate it."

"But we love it!"

"I think Ira's basically unisex."

"It's *definitely* unisex!"

They all laughed, Sandra sucked on the ice cube, dribbled it back into the glass. *Everyone wants to slap you in the face,* Elsie said to herself. She took a long drink, and then suddenly, Ira and Sandra had moved on, and she was alone again, the same conversations happening all around her, everyone living the dream. She wished she were alone in her cold classroom. She thought she could make out the sounds of a harp, but it was only the notes of a pop song. Someone had turned up the volume. She didn't want to think about her students, but she was always thinking about them, about students like Opal, probably doing homework on a Friday night, curled into a beanbag chair or in her bed, in a bedroom decorated in a style that seemed to indicate a much younger child slept there.

Elsie was sure Ira and Sandra were mostly joking. But she was getting desperate. And what if she did get published? What if her Y.A. novel became a best-seller, and someone wanted to interview her, would she still be claiming to be Ira Belman? Or would she come clean? Would they ask her if she had intended to shake up the publishing world? Were there awards for such things?

Of course, if she were still getting rejected, even with the Harvard degree, then she would know her novel in progress would never be good enough. She'd have definitive proof that she wasn't meant to be a writer. And then she could let it go, give up, spend her time watching old movies or cleaning her apartment, dusting the furniture, throw out the sweaty black turtleneck sweater. There was still time for her to live her life without the weight of trying to tell a coming-of-age story, the weight of building up a main theme, of getting to a resolution.

She could feel her cell phone vibrating against her body as she ordered another drink. She was trying to have a good time, thinking she might circulate, say hello, maybe find Ira and Sandra, right after she finished her beer. And maybe one or two more. She'd start looking for them when she had half a beer left, and that would be it. She'd stop after two more. Maybe three. The vibrations stopped, then started up again. Someone was trying to get through to her. ■

& WHAT'S LEFT

of the poet
who tires of pain

in an economy
of trauma?

What of the tongue
that craves a sweetness

to finish
the savoring?

Is there no room
for a sweet tooth

among the salt of the earth?
Or is it that the grain

of salt, which provokes
more than it provides,

sorely relies
on the sweet

release of melting
sugar to caramel?

Either way,
with too much

& not enough
of the other,

the tongue ceases
to taste

TANO RUBIO

CENZONTLE

El Anglo con cara de inocente nos arrancó la lengua.
—Gloria Anzaldúa

They wince
when they see me
circling overhead
to swoop & strike
con mi boca,
sharp like coils
of barbed
      wire

But you do what you can
to keep what's yours,
bonded by spit—
a nest of collected
twig, leaf,
      & trash

■ ■ ■

Out of the earth,
four hundred tongues
sprout a forest,
rising above the clouds
that dip between ridges,
spanning from la Sandia Crest
to Cumberland Plateau,
each word shading
the ground before
it falls, dissolved in the heat
      of the next syllable

Rustling in the dark of morning,
our echo stirs from veins
of leaves as the last breath
      of vowels

TANO RUBIO

BIRDS IN WAR

ELAINE NEIL ORR

With all of the bombing and explosions and smoke everywhere, the impact of all of that on birds and other wildlife can be so significant that it is hard to speculate on the extent… [I]t is like a web, like breaking glass and watching it shatter out through the whole pane.

—Mark Shieldcastle, "As War Rages on in Ukraine, Animals Are Caught in the Crossfire," *Pittsburgh Post-Gazette*, 21 March 2022

24 February 2022

I am at a writing residency in the foothills of Amherst, Virginia. I wake with morning light. Beyond my balcony, a wave of mountains emerge in lavender and mauve. Two doves come in for a soft landing on a tree ten feet away.

The air is cold and brisk. I dress for breakfast, check the news. Russia is invading Ukraine, I learn, and wish to unlearn. After breakfast, I take my computer and walk the pebble path to my studio at the barn where I spend the day writing, drinking tea, napping.

26 February 2022

After lunch, I leave my studio and walk back to the residence hall where the coffee bar is open all day. I pour coffee into my insulated pink mug, stir in sugar and creamer, head back to my studio. Budded jonquils are thick, sheaths still green. I doubt they will open before I leave in two weeks. Afternoon sun hits my back. I have a novel to finish.

27 February 2022

A Ukrainian woman and her parrot flee to Poland.

29 February 2022

A rainy day and chill. Late afternoon, bunched clouds break open at the horizon, sending light into my studio. I do yoga. On the way back to the residence hall for dinner, I pass a net of bushes. A blue jay squawks. Overhead a hawk circles.

After dinner, I check the news. A forty-mile Russian convoy has entered Ukraine, headed toward Kyiv.

1 March 2022

I walk among the boxwoods at Virginia Center for the Creative Arts, inhaling their resinous scent. Bluebirds fly overhead, zips of blue. They nest. I see them every time I visit this place. Bluebirds and mockingbirds, those scissor flyers, bombardiers.

Only later do I learn that ten Ukrainian civilians are killed and thirty-five wounded during a Russian bombardment of Kharkiv.

8 March 2022

I am home. Four cardinals roost in the crepe myrtle beyond my writing window. I'm on my second cup of coffee. My novel is with my agent and I'm unmoored. There's nothing I can do but start another one. Oh, there are other things I can do. Taxes, for example, clean out the attic, cart items to Goodwill, scrub the bathroom tile. What the people of Ukraine wouldn't give for an ordinary day.

9 March 2022

Wettish day but not gloomy. One cardinal in the crepe myrtle this morning. A black cat crosses the road. I wish it were a fox but it isn't. Reports that Russia will attack Odessa. Elderly people can't evacuate. Or perhaps they won't. Seven bears are transported by truck from the Kyiv zoo about four hundred miles to the west, traversing dangerous territory and passing through multiple checkpoints.

11 March 2022

A morning of writing, a walk with the dog. We run up on five chickens in a neighbor's yard. The dog spots them first. They peck in the grass, unperturbed. The chickens are large, brown and gray, full of their chickenness, their small heads turning to look, then back to pecking. I laugh at their oddity in our old suburb.

Ukrainians, still in their homes, shelter animals, chinchillas, cats, dogs, parrots.

My rhythm is still off since returning from VCCA. I want to sit with my coffee and look at the mountains. I don't want to shop for groceries or fix dinner. I keep going out to buy lunch, dinner, coffee and scones.

12 March 2022

Last night I filled the birdfeeder. Just before dawn, rain arrived, hard and whipping. Now four male cardinals flit and light in the crepe myrtle. I finish my first cup of coffee. The sun comes out, turning the limbs silver. A few yellow leaves still hang on the sugar maple, and we're in March. I hadn't noticed until today when sun after rain has set them glowing. Buds on the dogwood press to open. I can almost hear them straining.

Where are the birds in Kyiv? Isn't it nesting time for them too, just as it is in North Carolina? The turtle dove, the collared dove, the woodpecker, the red-backed shrike, the house sparrow?

A hard freeze predicted tonight. We cover budding hydrangeas with blankets.

In Marhalivka, a Russian rocket hit a man's house. Twelve people reside here: two grandchildren, two nieces, wife, daughter, sister, and others. Only he, Ihor Mazhayev, and his cat survive. He flees to a nearby town to seek shelter.[1]

13 March 2022

The hydrangea buds survive.

Environmental scientists have studied the effect of extended wars on birds: "[H]abitat degradation caused by the war may have also influenced FIDs [flight initiation distances], with birds in degraded or open habitats displaying potentially longer FIDs. While the mechanisms linking war and escape responses of birds remain unclear, war evidently ha[s] left legacies of behavioral responses in bird species."[2]

It's four p.m. in Kyiv, thirty-two degrees. By chance, it's thirty-two degrees in Raleigh at ten a.m.

---

1   Bethany Dawson. "Photo Shows a Ukrainian Man Clutching His Cat." *Business Insider*, 12 March 2022.
2   Jonathan Gnanapragasam. "Study Shows Civil War Left Long Lasting Trauma in Birds." *Groundviews: Journalism for Citizens.* 18 November 2021.

Our eight year-old granddaughter visits. She swings and climbs trees and throws Frisbees for the dog and then she comes in, throws her arms wide, "There are so many cardinals out there!" They blaze back and forth across our wide front yard because we're feeding them. Because the hardware store is open and not all of our money has been appropriated for our own survival. We have a car. The roads are neither shelled nor blocked.

At first Ukrainians evacuate with cats and dogs. But many dogs are left. Caretakers at shelters stay with animals, traumatized by bombings.

(I cannot control this writing. It is going to get away from me. There's too much.)

14 March 2022

9 a.m. Thirty-three degrees in Raleigh. 2:53 p.m. Forty-three degrees in Kiev. I go out early to fill the birdfeeders.

Inventory of birds that visit my front yard:

Northern Cardinal
Carolina Chickadee
Carolina Wren
Tufted Titmouse
American Crow
Red bellied Woodpecker
Blue Jay
Eastern Bluebird
American Robin
Downy Woodpecker
Eastern Towhee
Northern Mockingbird
American Goldfinch
House Finch
White-breasted Nuthatch

Sparrow
Eastern Phoebe
Pine Warbler
Dark-eyed Junco
Ruby-throated hummingbird
Barred Owl
Red-tailed Hawk

I walk the dog for an hour, hear an aircraft overhead. The sound does not send me for cover. Though by the time I get home, I have thoughts about nuclear disaster. In Nagasaki and Hiroshima birds burst into flames in midair when the U.S. dropped atomic bombs.

15 March 2022

Red-bellied woodpecker in the crepe myrtle this morning. A thrumming noise fills my ears. It comes from my own throat, a sound of joy.

Twenty days of war in Ukraine. Three million Ukrainian refugees.

Ukraine is home to 425 bird species. What birds are on the grounds of the Mariupol theater where children shelter when it is hit by Russian bombs and 300 Ukrainians die?

17 March 2022

A rainy morning and with the time change, it's gray at eight a.m. Yet a red cardinal bobs on a branch of the crepe myrtle. I hear its call through closed glass, even against the thunder.

Tonight we have two owls in our front yard. We hear them first, then walk out to see their dark bunched forms.

20 March 2022

The first bird in the crepe myrtle today is the female cardinal, then three male cardinals.

I correspond with a Ukrainian woman on Facebook. She posts pictures of crocuses in her yard. They are "hatching," she says. I've asked her about birds. She doesn't have time to answer between waiting for electricity to return, learning when groceries may reach a near-by store, and hiding in the basement when she and her children hear shelling. Still, in moments of quiet, she walks in the garden to observe the crocus.

Two chickadees arrive and depart the crepe myrtle. A bluebird arrives like a miracle.

Later, my Ukrainian friend, I'll call her L, posts a picture her elder son has drawn for me: a dove, in blues and yellows, for Ukraine. The family lives in a working-class region of Chernihiv Oblast, eighty miles from Kyiv. The town is surrounded by landmines. L isn't sure who placed them there. They lurk in fields where Ukrainians normally plant wheat and corn. A local checkpoint commander says "the front is everywhere" and waves his hand.[3] Could a mine be set off by a ground bird?

21 March 2022

L says the night was "very much" not quiet; sirens going off. In the morning when it is quiet, she goes out into the garden. She tells us that while the bees are alive, there is life. The national animal of Ukraine is the common nightingale, harbinger of spring. Nightingales winter in the dry savannahs of sub-Sahara Africa. Where are they now on their route? Are they flying over the desert, over Saudi Arabia? Iran? Have they arrived in Ukraine to clouds of ash and smoke rising from bombed cities?

In *Birding Babylon*, Jonathan Trouern-Trend writes about watching wood pigeons near the north pond on his base in Iraq. "A pair of F-16s came tearing down the runway with their afterburners going. The noise was incredible as they quickly disappeared into the sky. The birds were unfazed."[4] And yet, I cannot believe the birds in Mariupol are unfazed. Surely they have flown from the city and into surrounding woods.

24 March 2022

Rainy morning. A bird sings loudly out the window as I fix my coffee. Seven long notes, then eight, then five, then seven, eight, six, all the same note. The white-throat sparrow.

A month ago Ukrainians woke at 5:07 to sounds of explosions. Each day since has brought air-raid sirens and breaking glass. L calls Russia "terrorist country," firing on civilians in their apartments, pregnant women in hospitals, children in their beds. L prepares for her youngest son's seventh birthday. She spends days gathering the ingredients to make the cake. She cuts it into pieces, soaks it in cream, and tops it with chocolate icing.

The dogwood outside my window is frilly with white blossoms. Yesterday afternoon a squirrel emptied the feeder and this morning no bird alights on the crepe myrtle though one wheels by my window.

Has L served her cake? It's eight a.m. here, two p.m. in Ukraine.

In favorable conditions, birds in urban landscapes need green zones, riparian corridors, "linear protected lands composed of natural vegetation, or at least vegetation that is more natural than in surrounding areas"[5]

3   "Mine Warfare on Kyiv's Eastern Front." *France 24*. 3 March 2022.
4   Jonathan Truern-Trend. *Birding Babylon: A Soldier's Jounral from Iraq* (San Francisco: Sierra Club Books, 2006), 37.
5   Jamie Mason, Christopher Moorman, George Hess, Kristen Sinclair. "Designing Suburban Greenways to Provide Habitat for Forest-Breeding Birds," *Landscape and Urban Planning* 80 (2007), 153-64.

I read a paper on bird populations in Lviv, where cemeteries are a significant forested area for birds. The paper studies two areas: parks and cemeteries. Species richness in Ukrainian green space occurs during breeding season, which starts now, in March, and goes through July. What is the present state of forested areas in Lviv?

On the Raleigh greenway, I see great blue herons, cormorants, eagles, egrets.

Where are the birds this morning? I see not a one in the crepe myrtle. Loneliness creeps in and I wonder why I'm sad, what is amiss in my world? My throat is full. My chest feels hollowed out. Finally the cardinal shows up at nine o'clock.

26 March 2022

L reports that the Yasnogorodka family ecopark, not far from Makarov, in the Kiev region, is damaged by shelling. Many animals die; the aviaries, she says, simply burn down. She posts a photograph, the shells of buildings consumed in fire and beyond them a charcoal sky. The park owned three hundred ostriches. Did any escape? Imagine a thousand wings thrashing against enclosure.

Cardinals have taken over my crepe myrtle this morning. They fly, land, nod their heads, fly, return, consider, fly. A female stays longer. A purple finch alights. Here is a juvenile brown thrasher, large as a robin, chest puffed, white feathers painted in brown flecks, head cocked, eyeing my window. A chickadee appears, two tufted titmice land, peck, fly.

The crepe myrtle is still leaf-bare, the last tree to bud, offering an open view this chilly spring day.

Later I see a chipping sparrow in the yard, its reddish-brown cap giving it away. Though I pass close to its perch in a bush, it does not flee.

27 March 2022

We visit "Wings of the City," an installation of sculpture by Jorge Marin. Our granddaughter stands on tiptoes before two giant bronze wings, stretches her arms high, the city skyline behind her. For a moment, she flies.

Headlines:

"Blasts heard in Ukrainian cities as Russia intensifies attacks."

"Ukrainian intelligence says Moscow wants to carve up the country like North and South Korea" 'It's 2 p.m. in Kyiv. Here's What You Need to Know" (CNN).

"Concert Between Explosions provides respite in Kharkiv Subway Shelter" (*Washington Post*).

"Russia Intensifies Attacks, with Mariupol on the Brink" (*New York Times*).

Bombs fly.

29 March 2022

L's neighborhood is bombed and her home is damaged. The house next to hers is destroyed. She and her family are safe. How fare the yellow crocuses?

1 April 2022

L and her two boys flee their home for a safe place in Ukraine. She leaves her husband behind. For now, her garden is lost to her. I pull the blinds on my writing window. Still, I imagine the cardinal streaking by, the beating heart of the world. ∎

NOCTURNAL BONDAGE

Deep in
a wildwood
at dusk
one man

can take
another,
if not
by surprise,

by awe,
descending
the trunk
of a yew

a mystery
to be solved
in his
arms;

this sort
of furtive
tryst
and how

the fervent
dalliance
bound
to follow

                              can feel
                              at first
                              a burst
                              of shadows

                of seeds
                of dandelion
                fleet
                on blades

of wildgrass
an hour
to sundown
once one

                              has knelt
                              in fields
                              of white
                              and green

          and yellow
          and blown
          a dry
          stemmed

                    cloud
                    most of us
                    who often
                    kneel

have mostly
forgotten
or never
known,

                          unlike
                          this man
                          now
                          between

    a western
    redcedar
    and a cypress,
    bottomless

        and trussed
        to a fallen
        western
        hemlock

                    he embraces
                    while he
                    gnaws
                    its bark,

              driven
              to taste
              histories
              hidden

                                    in its many
                                    rings, who
                                    last Saturday
                                    convinced

        the stranger
        at Forget-Me-
        Never
        meadow disco

                        atop him now
                        to meet
                        tonight
                        for this,

                here, where,
                unnoticed
                and from a
                cone's throw,

below a pine
a buck and doe
onpeer
with seeming

                                    interest,
                                    but can
                                    a men-
                                    liked man

like me
wist
blacktail
proclivities?

JEREMY HALINEN

BOOK REVIEWS

Karen Salyer McElmurray. *Voice Lessons.* Oak Ridge,
Tenn.: Iris Press, 2021. 128 pages. Softcover. $20.00.

Reviewed by Julie Hagy

I sit down to finish reading Karen Salyer McElmurray's
Voice Lessons outside of a coffee house. A cool fall breeze
diltes the air of the coffee's smell but
carries the sound of voices from the
tables around me. Bits of conversation
float up, then off, into the air.

I read. I eavesdrop. It feels like
trespassing, to invite oneself to briefly
inhabit the lives of others. But that is
precisely what the reader is invited to
do in the sixteen essays that comprise
Voice Lessons. Some of the essays have
been previously published; others have
not. Each is like a conversation with a
life-long friend: there is no holding back. Not in McElmurray's
detailed exploration of cancer, nor the experience of growing
up in a home that was inhabited as much by her mother's
mental illness as it was her mother herself.

In the prologue, we view McElmurray at the front of her elementary school classroom. McElmurray writes, "Once some men came to our first-grade class, looking for a kid to be Little Miss Lynch. I was called up to the front with two other little girls, and they looked at all of us and then told me to sit down." It's succinctly delivered, striking and raw images like this that invite the reader to pause and sit not only with McElmurray, but with their own pasts and insecurities. We sit in the garage with her after school while she waits hours for her mother to clean the already clean house. Later, we are invited to witness her picking though chocolates for her mother at the nursing home. In "Elixir," her voice guides us unflinchingly, colostomy bag and all, through stage three colon cancer.

The essay motifs are recurring: family, Appalachia, search for self, exploration of childhood, a life of academia, loss. McElmurray writes of the infant she gave up for adoption, her fractured relationship with her mother, coal mining, teaching writing to college students.

Some of the unpublished essays were among my favorites. Take, for instance, "My Mother, Breathing," which describes loss in ecological and familial sense. In this essay, McElmurray eloquently explores the devastating effects of strip mining and mountaintop removal alongside her own mother's deteriorating health. "She sleeps in her clothes and keeps only half the bed made up, in case she needs to get up quick," writes McElmurray of her mother's growing fear and unease. She spends her visit to her mother's home trying to create familiarity and order in a world that is becoming increasingly unfamiliar and disconnected in her mother's failing memory. The land around her is on equal, uneven footing. McElmurray cites statistics on the environmental and human impacts of mountaintop removal and strip mining, a list that includes fractured foundations, desecrated land and poisoned waters, before succinctly stating, "I wish I knew how to stop it, this inevitable journey towards loss."

One of the most striking essays in the collection is "Strange Tongues," which won the Annie Dillard Award from the *Bellingham Review*. In the essay, McElmurray visits her mother in the nursing home. As her mother, suffering from Alzheimer's, struggles to remember her daughter's name, repeatedly asking her, "you think you're something don't you?", the author replays her childhood, remembering everything, from the exact chocolate confections her mother picked from the Whitman's Samplers boxes to the plastic covered couch she was not allowed to sit on. All the while, McElmurray is trying to reconcile her mother's question: what does she think she is? Painful and straightforward, the essay leaves a bittersweet aftertaste in the back of the reader's throat.

There are recurring scenes that play out in more than one essay: the aunt who found her husband dead in his car, a cousin's suicide. As stand-alone essays, I think the images are strong, but as a volume, the scenes lose the shock value the second or third time around.

McElmurray's poetic prose makes the writing itself savory. Some lines require pause, to stop and read again, to savor the depth. "I comb my hair to keep the world neat, but it doesn't help," she writes. Of her aunt, she writes, " She dreamed of one long highway, the way out she never took."

McElmurray's writing, while deeply personal, derives most of its power from its ability to connect to universal feeling. *Voice Lessons* contains themes that resonate with any person struggling to reconcile past with present. She wrestles the pain onto paper, and beautifully allows the reader to examine the construction of her voice, and perhaps their own. ∎

CAVE HILL CEMETERY

I come to your grave
to speak to the stone,
     as white as the day
    we buried you.

My last view was flat,
color bound by brushwork
     and the rose dyes
     they run through—

so I turn to library
light, you ripe inside
     owl-eyed glasses
     eclipsed with text

and think of caramel
breath, your heel-toe
     fall along the hall
     to wind our walnut clock,

another grandfather—
who chimes at off times
     of the day, your way
     of staying relevant?

We chose a plot where
a great magnolia hovers,
     she mothers the bees
     and white-winged moths,

who rustle among sage
blades and mustard
       tongued violets—they
       crown your granite,

like strident purple
planets—we plant a holly
       at your head, ever
       green to chaperone,

may she bear fruit
this winter and redden
       your white,
       white stone.

MAUD WELCH

CONTRIBUTORS

Wendell Berry, an essayist, novelist, and poet, has been honored with the T. S. Eliot Prize, the Aiken Taylor Award in Modern American Poetry, the John Hay Award of the Orion Society, and the Dayton Literary Peace Prize Richard C. Holbrooke Distinguished Achievement Award, among others. In 2010, he was awarded the National Humanities Medal by President Barack Obama. Berry lives with his wife, Tanya Berry, on their farm in Henry County, Kentucky.

Marisa P. Clark is a queer writer who grew up on the Mississippi Gulf Coast and came out in Atlanta. Her prose and poetry appear in *Shenandoah, Cream City Review, Nimrod, Epiphany, Foglifter, Free State Review, Rust + Moth, Texas Review, Sundog Lit, Air/Light,* and elsewhere. *Best American Essays 2011* recognized her creative nonfiction among its Notable Essays. A fiction reader for *New England Review*, she lives in New Mexico.

Monic Ductan's writing has appeared in *Southeast Review, Shenandoah, Appalachian Review, South Carolina Review,* and various other journals. Her essay "Fantasy Worlds," published in *Appalachian Review*, was listed as notable in *Best American Essays 2019*. She lives in Cookeville, Tennessee, where she teaches at Tennessee Tech University.

Paul Gilroy is one of the foremost theorists of race and racism working and teaching in the world today. Author of foundational and highly influential books such as *There Ain't No Black in the Union Jack* (1987), *The Black Atlantic: Modernity and Double Consciousness* (1993), *Against Race* (2000), *Postcolonial Melancholia* (2005) and *Darker Than Blue* (2010) alongside numerous key articles, essays and critical interventions, Gilroy's is a unique voice that speaks to the centrality and tenacity of racialized thought and representational practices in the modern world. He lives in London, UK.

Julie Hagy is a writer and journalist from Virginia. Her work has appeared in AAA travel publications, *5280 Magazine, Blue Ridge Outdoors,* and *Daily Camera*, among others.

What Other Choice by **Jeremy Halinen** (he/they) won the 2010 Exquisite Disarray First Book Poetry Contest. They are a classically trained ad libitum pianist and vocalist and a past/present/future life investigator. Halinen's poems appear or will in periodicals including *Cimarron Review, Court Green, Greensboro Review, Los Angeles Review, Meridian, Notre Dame Review, Poet Lore, Sentence,* and *Tampa Review* and in anthologies including *Best Gay Poetry 2008; I Go to the Ruined Place: Contemporary Poems in Defense of Global Human Rights; Collective Brightness: LGBTIQ Poets on Faith, Religion & Spirituality; A Face to Meet the Faces: An Anthology of Contemporary Persona Poetry; Pale Fire: New Writing on the Moon;* and volume 3 of *Aurora - The Allegory Ridge Poetry Anthology.*

bell hooks (née Gloria Jean Watkins) was among the leading public intellectuals of her generation. Her writings cover a broad range of topics including gender, race, teaching, and contemporary culture across the literary genres and include the seminal *Ain't I a Woman? Black Women and Feminism* and, more recently, *Appalachian Elegy: Poetry and Place.* She taught at Yale University, Oberlin College, and the City University of New York, and served as Distinguished Professor in Residence in Appalachian Studies at Berea College.

Silas House is the *New York Times* bestselling author of seven novels, one book of creative nonfiction, and three plays. His writing has appeared in the *New York Times, The Atlantic, The Advocate, Time, Garden & Gun,* and other publications. A former commentator for NPR's *All Things Considered,* House is the winner of the Nautilus Award, the Storylines Prize from the NAV/New York Public Library, an E. B. White Honor, and many other awards.

Qrescent Mali Mason is an Assistant Professor of Philosophy at Haverford College and currently serves as the President of the International Simone de Beauvoir Society. From 2015-2018, she taught in the Women's and Gender Studies Department at Berea College, where she solidified a commitment to the value of interdisciplinarity and intersectional theorizing through teaching and researching in Gender and Sexuality Studies and African American Studies, in addition to existentialism and phenomenology, feminist philosophy, critical race philosophy, and ethics and social/political philosophy. Her most recent writings include "#BlackGirlMagic as Resistant Imaginary," and "We Feel Grateful and Alive to be Doing This Work Together: Phenomenological Reflections on a 2020 Summer of Feminist Research Across Difference," and she is currently working on a book manuscript titled *On Ambiguity*.

Caroline McTeer is a writer of fiction and nonfiction, a thirty-one-year-old breast cancer survivor, a four on the Enneagram, a member of the Democratic Socialists of America, a runner, and a lover of television and travel. She has been published in *The Bitter Southerner*, *Sojourners*, and elsewhere.

Rita Mookerjee is the Ida B. Wells-Barnett Postdoctoral Fellow at DePaul University. Her poetry is featured in *Juked, Hobart Pulp, New Orleans Review, the Offing*, and the *Baltimore Review*.

Darnell L. Moore is currently Vice President of Inclusion Strategy for Content and Marketing at Netflix. A prolific writer, he has been published in various media outlets including the *New York Times, Vanity Fair, MSNBC, The Guardian, Quartz, Playboy, Huffington Post, EBONY, The Root, The Advocate, OUT Magazine, Gawker, VICE, Guernica, Thought Catalog, Good Men Project,* and others. Moore is the author of the 2019 Lambda Literary Award nominated memoir, *No Ashes in the Fire: Coming of Age Black & Free in America*.

Elaine Neil Orr is professor of English at North Carolina State University and serves on the faculty of the low-residency MFA in Writing program at Spalding University. Author of *A Different Sun*, two scholarly books, and the memoir *Gods of Noonday: A White Girl's African Life*, she has been a featured speaker and writer-in-residence at numerous universities and conferences and is a frequent fellow at the Virginia Center for the Creative Arts. She grew up in Nigeria.

Leah Brennan Renberg received an MFA in Fiction from Chatham University. She has contributed poetry, short fiction, and essays to journals such as *Burrow Press Review, Voices from the Attic, Fourth River,* and *Northeast Magazine*.

tano rubio is a writer and teacher from East Tennessee. He has published or forthcoming work in *Recenter Press, Bodega, Rattle*,

Southern Humanities Review, and *Reckoning: Tennessee Writers On 2020*. You can find him online: @tanorubio_ .

Shannon St. Armand lives in the Pennsylvania town in which she grew up and writes poetry in-between potty training and walking in the woods with her three small, tornado children. Most recently, her work has been published in *Relief Journal* and in *Dappled Things*. You can follow her on Instagram @shannonsaintarmand.

Gloria Steinem is a writer, lecturer, political activist, and feminist organizer. She has spent decades traveling in this and other countries as an organizer and lecturer and is a frequent media spokeswoman on issues of equality. She is particularly interested in the shared origins of sex and race caste systems, gender roles and child abuse as roots of violence, non-violent conflict resolution, the cultures of indigenous peoples, and organizing across boundaries for peace and justice. She lives in New York City.

Dr. Linda Strong-Leek serves as the Provost of Haverford College. She is a Professor of Africana and Gender and Sexuality Studies. Before joining Haverford, she served as the Provost of Berea College. She also served as the first Vice President for Diversity and Inclusion at Berea, as well as the Associate Vice-President for Academic Affairs for seven years. Dr. Strong-Leek has traveled abroad extensively, particularly in the Caribbean and Africa. She also enjoys traveling with students, and has, in conjunction with Berea College faculty and staff, traveled with students to Ghana and Jamaica. She was a Fulbright Senior Scholar at the University of Zimbabwe in Harare, in 1998.

Maud Welch holds a BA in English Literature from Bates College and is currently pursuing an MFA at Spalding University. She resides in her hometown of Louisville, Kentucky. Her work has been published or is forthcoming in *Rust + Moth, New Ohio Review* and *New Delta Review.*

Crystal Wilkinson, Kentucky's Poet Laureate, is the award-winning author of *Perfect Black*, a collection of poems, and three works of fiction: *The Birds of Opulence, Water Street, and Blackberries,*

Blackberries. She is the recipient of a 2022 NAACP Image Award for Outstanding Poetry, a 2021 O. Henry Prize, a 2020 USA Artists Fellowship, and a 2016 Ernest J. Gaines Prize for Literary Excellence. Her work has appeared in numerous journals and anthologies including *The Atlantic, The Kenyon Review, STORY, Agni Literary Journal, Emergence, Oxford American* and *Southern Cultures. Praise Song for the Kitchen Ghosts*, a culinary memoir, is forthcoming in August 2023. She currently teaches at the University of Kentucky where she is Associate Professor of English in the MFA in Creative Writing Program.

www.ingramcontent.com/pod-product-compliance
Lightning Source LLC
Chambersburg PA
CBHW070601180626
46817CB00005B/1941

* 9 7 8 1 4 6 9 6 7 2 4 6 5 *